MYTHS OF
THE RED CHILDREN
AND
INDIAN HERO TALES

COLLECTED BY
GILBERT L. WILSON

ILLUSTRATED BY
FREDERICK N. WILSON

ONAGOCAG PUBLISHING EDITION

With an introduction by
Wyatt R. Knapp

ONAGOCAG PUBLISHING CO.
WINTER HAVEN, FL & SAUGATUCK, MI
"OH-NAH-GO-SHOG"

INTRODUCTION

My father was the one who did it. I was about seven or eight years old, loved the woods and water, loved Indian crafts and lore, loved reading. On a day when I had expressed the desire for something new to read, my dad went to his room and after looking over the titles, he took a slender brick-red volume from his book shelf and handed it to me with a smile.

As we thumbed through the book together I saw the kinds of things that had stirred me even before that young age. Beaded leather goods, tepees, moccasins, turtle shell rattles, arrows, feathers, stone knives, American Indians. After a few words from Dad about my responsibility for caring for this very old book, and my assurance that I would give it right back after I was done reading it, I was off to my room. Nestled in my bed by the window, with the light of a cheery sunny afternoon splashing across the pages, I was lost—completely immersed—in a world of ice giants, magic wigwams, and traditional American Indian crafts and lore.

That was my introduction to the book *Myths of the Red Children*. Over the years I would often ask my dad to lend it to me, always taking care of it and returning it when I was done. When I was grown, and a father myself, my dad gave the book to me, and when my children were old enough I shared it with them. They too were captivated by the stories. The multigenerational attraction of that little book, and its later companion, *Indian Hero Tales*, speaks not only to the spiritual nature, depth of culture and wit of the oral traditions of the American Indians, but also to the talent and sensitivity of the man who collected, retold and published them.

Gilbert L. Wilson

Gilbert Livingstone Wilson, oldest son of Samuel and Mary Wilson, was born in October of 1869 in Springfield, Clark County, Ohio. From a very young age Wilson was interested in the history, stories and crafts of the American Indians. After his education at Lake Forest and Wittenberg Colleges in Ohio he enrolled at Princeton Theological Seminary, completing his studies there in 1899. Then, as a Presbyterian minister, he received a pastorate in Mandan, North Dakota, where he was excited to find he lived near Indians. The passion he had felt for Indian life and culture had never waned. Living so near them inspired him to collect their stories and to record how they lived and what their craft and tool cultures were like. His health was such that his doctor had advised him to "purchase a pony and a gun and seek the open." Wilson found that a much more interesting way to follow doctor's orders was to work outdoors, researching and collecting information on the Indians and their way of life. Living among them and sharing their lives and traditions seemed the best medicine. Besides, Wilson cared about these people. He felt an urgency to help protect and preserve the culture and heritage of what he saw as a vanishing race.

In order to illustrate his research, Wilson enlisted the help of his brother, Frederick N. Wilson. From 1905 to 1918 they worked closely together, collecting stories and information on Hidatsa daily life and culture from the people themselves, and in particular a woman named Buffalo Bird Woman, her son Goodbird, and her brother, Wolf Chief. The Wilson brothers and this family became so close that both Gilbert and Frederick were formally adopted into the Buffalo Woman's clan, making them her sons.

In 1910 Gilbert L. Wilson enrolled in graduate school at the University of Minnesota with a major in anthropology. His thesis was *Agriculture of the Hidatsa Indians: An Indian Interpretation.* Lacking the agriculturalist's educational background, Wilson had the idea that his thesis would address its subject matter in a way more true to his role as an ethnologist. He decided his thesis would use the agricultural material culture of the Hidatsa to show something of the inner soul or life of these indigenous people. Its published title was *Agriculture of the Hidatsa: An Indian Interpretation.* This remarkable work was later published by Wilson in 1917. Several other editions have been published in the decades that followed—a testament to its popularity and the value of its subject matter to this day.

For Gilbert Wilson, the time spent with his adopted family collecting stories and information and working on his thesis was fondly recalled in later years as "one of the pleasantest experiences" of his life.

An Extraordinary Legacy

Wilson's ethnographic work continued long after the publication of his thesis. At one point he held the position of "Field Collector for the American Museum of History in New York." Still, that Wilson saw himself first and foremost as a pastor seems evident. After his graduation from seminary he was listed as such in every U.S. census record for the rest of his life. There is no mention in them of the decades he spent working as an ethnologist and anthropologist. But given his incredible life's work of manuscripts, notes, and information, it would be difficult for anyone to ignore his contribution to the understanding and preservation of American Indian traditions and culture. Wilson's material in the holdings of the University of North Dakota alone are stunning in their scope and depth.

Wilson's work in the field has been described as "an enormous record of published writings, notes, photos, and letters" and "a boon to historians, archaeologists and other anthropologists interested in past cultures." Ethnologist Robert Lowie once wrote that not only was Wilson a keen observer, but also that Wilson's recording of ethnological detail was such that Lowie could not hope to compete with him. French anthropologist Claude Lévi-Strauss, a man considered the father of modern anthropology, referenced Wilson's *Hidatsa Eagle Trapping* as "one of the finest masterpieces in all anthropological literature." Wilson's work has been described as an extensive and accurate history of traditional American Indian culture.

By the time of his passing at his home in St. Paul, Minnesota, on June 8th, 1930, Wilson had left so much ethnological information that much of his material is still waiting for publication to this day. It lies in the collections of private colleges and museums in various states throughout the country, most notably North Dakota, Minnesota, and New York. Only recently have attempts been made to sift through the sheer volume of his collections and materials in order to start the process of publishing the rest of his work.

Myths of the Red Children and Indian Hero Tales

Gilbert L. Wilson published several books intended for the general reading public. Two of them, *Goodbird The Indian, His Story, Told by Himself* (1914) and *Waheene: an Indian Girl's Story, Told by Herself* (1921) were extremely important ethnological works. But the publication of *Myths Of The Red Children* and *Indian Hero Tales,* both collections of stories reflecting American Indian oral storytelling traditions, stand out for their popular appeal to young and old alike.

Of the two books, *Myths of the Red Children*, with its collection of stories from various tribes and regions of North America, is more suitable for younger children. There are, however, a few stories that deal with difficult subjects. For instance, the cautionary tale "The Little Fawn" and the clever and engaging legend "The Fisher Who Let Out Summer" include the death of a loved one. "The Flying Head" gives a scary personification of a whirlwind, or cyclone, and tells how its own actions led to its destruction. However none of these stories should be any more challenging to children than the old classic fairy tales or even most of the Disney movies we watched as kids. Parents can preview the collection in order to decide which stories to share with their children.

Indian Hero Tales, the natural sequel to *Myths of the Red Children*, seems more suited for older children. Rather than give stories from various tribes and regions, *Indian Hero Tales* concentrates solely on the oral tradition of the Indians of the Abnaki Confederacy who lived in the area of the Atlantic coast between the northern United States and Canada. When read in sequence, the stories in *Indian Hero Tales* give a cohesive narrative depicting the adventures of the Abnaki Indian hero Glooskap. These stories offered the Abnaki explanations for why the world is the way it is and provided the basis for many of their beliefs and traditions. The Abnaki creation story is memorably told and preserved in *Indian Hero Tales*.

Both books feature several pages of valuable explanatory notes, as well as copiously illustrated supplemental craft sections. Those wanting to recreate traditional Indian crafts will find Wilson's friendly presentation style helpful and encouraging as they experience the satisfaction of making and using tools and accoutrements featured in the stories. Clear instructions reveal Wilson's first-hand experience and understanding of their methods of manufacture. Ideas for how to "make do" with more contemporary materials or methods, when the need arises, gives one a glimpse into the resourcefulness of the man who once wrote about how he had made "good arrowheads" out of flint and glass using an old bone toothbrush handle as a "chipping tool."

Reading Wilson In Proper Context

When reading *Myths of the Red Children* and *Indian Hero Tales*, one is given the opportunity to experience how English language usage and grammar has changed in the last one hundred years. Wilson often writes with a charming turn of phrase. Take for example the following:

> *"When he had done hunting, Glooskap would say, 'Dogs grow small!' and the wolves would become small as before."*

and:

> *"... Mikchich was stout hearted. He bethought him of his flight over the wigwam."*

The poetic spirit of Wilson's language is reminiscent of Longfellow's *Hiawatha*. The contemporary reader soon falls naturally into the pleasing cadence and rhythms of the written word at the turn of the twentieth century.

Wilson possessed a keen vocabulary. For example, in one story he describes how the waves went *"plashing"* by. This could easily be mistaken for a typographical error, as one might assume he had meant to write *"splashing."* However, although not a common word these days, *plash* means to "dash a liquid upon or against" or "a sound like water splashing."

Wilson's books have become historic examples of early American literature. Care has been taken to ensure that the stories in this edition are presented with the language and vocabulary as originally published.

It is perhaps here that a word to the reader about the evolution of words or terms used in anthropology and science would be appropriate. In every language, words and their meanings evolve. Many of us have seen this in our own lifetimes. Etymological dictionaries are filled with examples of word and phrase evolution. Words that meant one thing long ago mean something quite different now.

One rule of word evolution seems to be that if a word has more than one meaning, the less controversial meaning of the word will invariably be supplanted by the more controversial one. It would serve us well, as conscientious readers of older literature, to take into account the context of the original writer's experience in the time he lived—what their knowledge and culture was, how the words were used in their time. To do so helps us understand the author's true intent and brings clarity and fairness to the text.

Readers will no doubt find instances where a word or phrase used by Wilson may seem, in today's vernacular, "politically incorrect." For example, at one point in one of his forewords he speaks of "barbarians". This can be a culturally charged word in our time, especially when referring to American Indians. However, as a practitioner of ethnological science, Wilson is using the term correctly for the time in which he lived. While we now commonly hold the definition of "barbarian" to mean "brutal, cruel and insensitive," one of the actual dictionary definitions of the word holds a clue to how Wilson would have meant it. It says, "a member of a people considered by those of another nation or group to have a primitive civilization." Even that definition contains the problem word "primitive." But as my website, *The History and Primitive Technology Page*, points out, "primitive" is defined as "of or pertaining to an earliest or original stage or state." It does not mean less intelligent, or less creative, or less inventive.

Wilson's writings should be viewed in the context of the scientific disciplines he represented, and what the words he used meant at the time he wrote. In addition, his works should be seen in light of an entire lifetime spent researching, promoting, and celebrating American Indians and their culture. We need only read his own words to understand how he felt about indigenous Americans. In his books and writings he repeatedly pointed out that the things he shared belonged to the Indians. Over and over he claimed no credit other than collecting the information and translating it into English. He was careful to let his readers know that bits of Indian philosophy and shrewd or humorous observations found in the narratives were not his but his "informants'." Wilson was also consistent throughout his life in his pleas for better appreciation of the American Indian race. His style of anthropology has been described as "enlightened and sensitive."

The Art of Frederick N. Wilson

Both books are illustrated throughout with the art of Frederick N. Wilson, whose drawings go far beyond merely illustrating the tales. Tools, clothing and accoutrements are shown with great attention to detail. His pen and ink renderings even show the scar patterns of flintknapped stone and the lashings on tomahawks and tools. Beadwork, fringe and decorations are all faithfully rendered. Many of his drawings are so detailed they could be used as templates for the creation of authentic replicas.

The artist skillfully depicts the humor, irony, sadness or lesson of the story. He has a knack for capturing emotion. In *Indian Hero Tales* the drawing of a young Glooskap sitting in the darkness, alone by a fire, shows such sensitivity and understanding about the feelings of grief related in the story. Another drawing shows a lovely Zuni girl with shell necklace and earrings. The look on her face is one of such calm, grace and beauty.

Some details become evident only after close or frequent viewing. Things like rabbits with ears that are drawn to look like eagle feathers, cloud formations in the shape of an animal, or a snake used as a border for a picture.

Frederick Wilson was playful with his use of space on the page. The action or story told in the drawing often tumbles down the sides or extends into the text, lending interest and uniqueness to the book. Another trademark of his style was the way he featured elements of everyday Indian life in his drawings. One can tell his heart was with those whose oral traditions he was illustrating. In perfect harmony with his brother Gilbert's skillful translations, Frederick's drawings help to educate the reader about Indian life.

Gilbert L. Wilson was more than just a collector and translator of the stories. He was a respectful and caring conservator whose talent at shaping them into English for his readers was unexcelled. The combination of Gilbert's translations and his brother Frederick's drawings has secured these books a lasting place in the annals of ethnological and popular literature.

A Definitive Centennial Edition

Original copies of *Myths of the Red Children* in "very good" or better condition can be expensive and are becoming harder to find. The same is true of *Indian Hero Tales*. As the two are natural literary companions, it seemed logical to publish them as a combined hard-cover edition. Wilson's fine collection of American Indian stories and crafts, along with his brother Frederick's drawings, have now been preserved in an attractive new and enlarged format.

It has been over one hundred years since the publication of *Myths of the Red Children*. The centennial anniversary of the release of *Indian*

Hero Tales is fast approaching. These two books have long been recognized as important contributions to the preservation of American Indian culture and lore. The time is right to reintroduce these kinds of quality stories, and the traditional cultures they represent, to a new generation.

Onagocag Publishing is proud to present this definitive centennial edition. May it find favor with you and yours for many years to come.

- Wyatt R. Knapp, Aug. 2012
Saugatuck, Michigan

BOOK ONE

MYTHS OF THE RED CHILDREN

CONTENTS

BOOK TWO

INDIAN HERO TALES

CONTENTS

BOOK ONE

MYTHS OF
THE RED CHILDREN

FOREWORD

by Gilbert L. Wilson

All American children listen with delight to our fine old English fairy tales. Few of us, even of maturer years, do not own a kindly feeling for Cinderella or heroic Jack of the Bean Stalk.

But these tales were brought to us from Europe, and they have never wholly lost the marks of their foreign origin. Who has not longed for a fairy lore of our own — one native to our broad America.

Such a lore we have. Among our Indian tribes still lingers a rich body of myth and folk tale, breathing all the freshness of our rugged forests and mountains.

These tales have dignity. Like every barbarian, the Indian peopled the world with wonder-folk — gods and monsters, ghosts and spirits. His myths, therefore, give us a glimpse into his thought. They are his oral literature, the wisdom of the elder-men, handed down by mouth.

Many myths are sacred and were believed as firmly as white children believe the beautiful story of Joseph. Others were told to amuse, or, like fables, were made to teach morals to the young.

The long winter evenings were the season for story-telling.

About the lodge fire then gathered men and women, youths and maidens. Reverently they listened as some aged story-teller rehearsed the doings of the gods.

The myths in this little volume have been chosen for their quaintness and beauty. They are taken from the lore of several tribes.

Let us hope they will give to little reading folk a kindly feeling for a noble but vanishing race.

One of the objects in collecting these stories is to help children learn to read. All little folk enjoy simple, imaginative tales, and what they enjoy they will read.

The stories contain much information about Indian life and customs that is of value to an American child. Many pages of our history become plainer to one who knows something of Indian life.

A brief explanatory note accompanies every story. It is intended that each note shall explain some custom or belief of Indian life or some fact of woodcraft mentioned in the story.

Children are natural mimics and keenly enjoy dramatic interpretation. The reading of the myths may be supplemented by a simple dramatization. Make a tepee, after directions on page 103, large enough for a child to enter; set up in a convenient corner; hang an iron pot before, on a simple tripod of three sticks.

In the preparation of these stories the author claims no credit but that of rewriting them for little folk's tastes. The stories are true examples of Indian folk-lore, and are very old. The following sources and authorities are acknowledged: Frank H. Cushing's *Zuñi Folk Tales,* for "Little Ugly Boy," "The Turkey Maiden"; Charles G. Leland's *Algonquin Legends of New England,* for "Wuchowson the Wind Blower," "Glooskap and the Winter Giant," "The Magic Wigwam," "Why the Baby says 'Goo'," "The Good Giants"; Silas Rand's *Micmac Legends,* for "Little Scar Face"; "Omaha and Ponka Texts," translated by James Dorsey (Vol. VI, *Contributions to North American Ethnology)*, for "Why Turkeys have Red Eyes," "The Sun Man and the Moon," "How the Little Rabbit snared the Sun," "The Little Fawn"; Schoolcraft's *Hiawatha Myths,* for "The Fisher who let out Summer"; W. W. Canfield's *Legends of the Iroquois,* for "Old Winter Man and the Spring Maiden"; J. W. Powell, in *First Annual Report of the Bureau of American Ethnology,* for "The Rainbow Snake"; Mrs. E. A. Smith, in *Second Annual Report of the Bureau of American Ethnology,* for "The Flying Head"; James Mooney's "Myths of the Cherokee," in *Nineteenth Annual Report of the Bureau of American Ethnology,* for "The Little Ice Man," "The Wren."

Acknowledgment is also made of the courtesy of Mr. J. D. Allen, of Mandan; of the late Honorable J. V. Brower, of St. Paul; of Mr. E. R. Steinbrueck, Field Officer of the State Historical Society of

North Dakota; and of the kindly help of many humble Indian friends among the Standing Rock and Fort Berthold Reservation bands.

Illustrations in this volume are by the author's brother, Mr. Frederick N. Wilson. Care has been taken to make the drawings archeologically correct for each tribe.

"WHA-A-AH!" HE ROARED. "IT IS THE DEATH GHOST!"

Original frontispiece from the 1907 edition

···MYTHS OF···
THE RED CHILDREN

RETOLD BY

GILBERT L. WILSON, Ph.D.

ILLUSTRATED BY FREDERICK N. WILSON

GINN & COMPANY

BOSTON · NEW YORK · CHICAGO · LONDON

Original title page from the 1907 edition

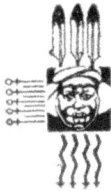

I

LITTLE UGLY BOY

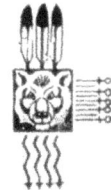

A long time ago in Eagle village lived an old woman and her little grandson. The little boy was very ugly. His skin was of the color of blue paint. His eyes were crooked and squinting. His nose was twisted over to one side. On his head grew ugly red things like red peppers.

He was so ugly that no one liked to look at him. Even the village children would not have him for a playmate.

"Go away, little Ugly Boy!" they would say. "We do not like to play with you. You are too ugly."

At that time the people of Eagle village ate piñon nuts and grass seeds. They dried the nuts in heaps and put them away in

ZUÑI GIRL GRINDING MEAL

store-rooms built of stone. The grass seeds they ground up into meal.

Near the village stood the nut trees in a grove, and there the grass seeds also grew. But one year, when the time came for the nuts and seeds to ripen, no one dared go to gather them.

A wicked old Bear had come down from the mountains and had his den in a thicket near the grove. Whenever any one went out to gather nuts or seeds the Bear would come roaring out of his den. Some of the people he killed. Others he hurt or drove away. Everybody was afraid of him.

One day little Ugly Boy came into the house feeling hungry. His grandmother was sitting on the floor making clay pots.

"Grandmother, I am going out to gather nuts and grass seeds," he said.

"O grandson, do not do that! The wicked bear will catch you! He will eat you up!" cried his grandmother.

ZUÑI POTTERY

4

But little Ugly Boy was not afraid. He put a basket on his back and went out to the place where the nut trees grew.

The ripe nuts had fallen from the trees until they covered the ground. Little Ugly Boy sat down on the grass to eat some of the nuts. He cracked the shells with his teeth and munched the rich kernels. They were very sweet.

Suddenly there came a crashing through the trees. Little Ugly Boy looked up. There was the wicked old Bear coming straight at him.

"Woof!" roared the Bear. "What are you doing in my grass patch? What are you doing among my nut trees?"

"I am eating nuts," said little Ugly Boy. He was not a bit afraid.

"You must go away! These nuts are mine," growled the Bear.

"No, they are not yours; they are mine," said little Ugly Boy.

This made the Bear angry.

"Yes, they are mine! If you do not go I will tear you to pieces! I am bigger and braver than you," he roared.

"No, they are not yours, and you are *not* braver than I am," said little Ugly Boy, laughing.

"Yes, I am braver," roared the Bear.

"No, you are not," said little Ugly Boy, "and I shall prove it. Let us try to scare one another. First you try to scare me, then I will try to scare you. The one who scares the other shall have the nuts and grass seeds."

The Bear laughed very much when he heard this.

"Ha, ha!" he roared. "Think of a little fellow like you scaring *me!* Indeed, I am very willing to try."

So little Ugly Boy sat on the ground eating nuts, while the Bear ran away and hid again in his den.

After a while there came a loud roar from the thicket. The Bear rushed out and came crashing through the trees straight at the little Ugly Boy.

"Wha-a-ah!" he roared. "Woof! I'll eat you up! I'll eat you up!"

As he ran he tossed great clouds of dust in the air. He broke off branches and knocked over young trees with his paws.

But little Ugly Boy only laughed. He was not afraid.

The Bear was surprised.

ZUÑI LADDER

"Little Ugly Boy, you are brave," he growled. "I did not scare you a bit. Now run away and see if you can scare *me.*"

Little Ugly Boy ran home again as the Bear bade him. His grandmother still sat on the floor, making clay pots. As he came down the ladder from the roof, he called out to her: "Grandmother, the wicked Bear tried to scare me, but I was not afraid. Now I shall try to scare him. Come and paint my face; make me look terrible."

"Yes, grandson, I will do as you say," answered his grandmother.

She put away the clay pots and went over to the fireplace. Here she made a little heap of ashes and drew some soot out of the chimney. With the soot she painted one side of little Ugly Boy's face a deep black. The other side she painted white with ashes. When she had finished his face was terrible.

ZUÑI FIREPLACE

She then gave him an old stone ax.

"Grandson, take this ax," she said. "It is magic. If you strike anything with it the ground will rumble and shake. Everybody will be frightened."

Little Ugly Boy took the stone ax and ran again to the place where the nut trees grew.

The Bear was sitting on the ground eating nuts. Little Ugly Boy ran at him, crying,

"He! he! he! he! he! he! tooh!"

As he ran he struck a hollow tree with his stone ax. The tree split and fell down with a crash. The earth heaved and shook.

ZUÑI CHIMNEY

Rocks rolled about upon the ground. The wicked old Bear jumped straight up into the air. He thought the earth was going to sink under him.

Then he saw little Ugly Boy's face. One half was painted black with soot, and the other half white with ashes. The Bear had never seen such a terrible sight.

Little Ugly Boy struck another tree with his stone ax. There was an awful rumble. The ground shook as if it would fly to pieces.

Little Ugly Boy was now quite close to the Bear. Once more he struck a tree with his stone ax.

At once there was a terrible earthquake. Trees fell down upon the ground. Rivers rose out of their beds and overflowed their banks. Mountains shook as if they would topple over.

STONE AX

The wicked old Bear was so frightened that he fell down and rolled upon his back. He was scared almost to death.

"Wha-a-ah!" he roared. "It is the Death Ghost! If I do not run away he will kill me." And he jumped to his feet and ran back to the mountains as fast as he could run.

Little Ugly Boy filled his basket with nuts and grass seeds and went back home again. He was very happy.

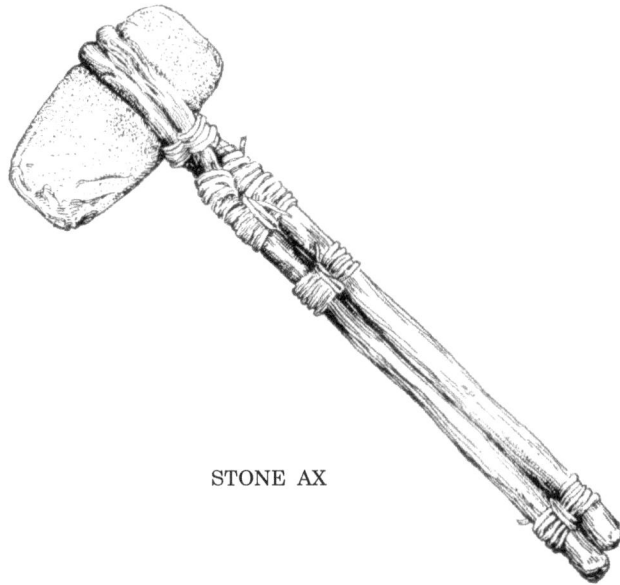

"Grandmother," he cried, "I scared the wicked old Bear. He was terribly frightened. He ran back again to the mountains!"

Then he went up to the roof of the house and called out: "Ho, you people of Eagle village! Now you can gather nuts and grass seeds. The wicked old Bear has gone. I frightened him away with my stone ax."

II

WHY TURKEYS HAVE RED EYES

In a thicket on a river bank stood the lodge of a little gray Rabbit. His father and mother were dead and his old Rabbit grandmother kept house for him. They were very poor. Often they had hardly enough to eat.

One day they sat down to dinner very hungry. All they had to eat was a little handful of parched corn.

"Grandmother, this will not do. I must go hunting and kill some meat," said the little Rabbit.

His grandmother smiled at this.

"Grandson, you are too little. You are not big enough to hunt game," she said.

But the little Rabbit took his game bag and started bravely over the prairie. By and by he saw a flock of Turkeys. They were

OTO LODGE, OR TEPEE

feeding among some arrow weeds.

"Oho!" thought the little Rabbit; "how fat the Turkeys are! But how shall I catch them?"

He sat down on the ground awhile and thought. At last he took off his robe and filled it full of dry grass. He then rolled it up into a bundle.

"Perhaps now I can catch the Turkeys," he said.

He put the bundle on his back and began to run. As he came near, the Turkeys raised their heads up out of the

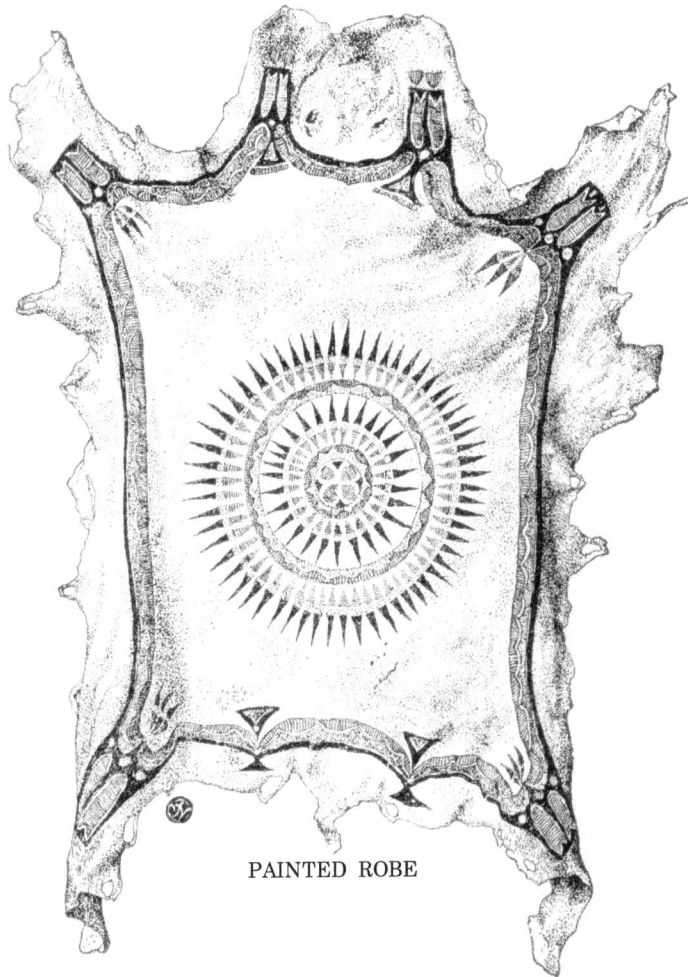

PAINTED ROBE

weeds. They were surprised to see him running with a bundle on his back.

"Ho, little brother! why are you running so fast?" asked an old Turkey.

"Because the villagers are going to give a dance. They wish me to sing for them. I am in a great hurry. The songs are in this bundle on my back," answered the little Rabbit.

"Oho! he says he has songs. How wonderful!" gobbled all the Turkeys.

WILD TURKEY

Then they called out to the little Rabbit: "Little brother, come and sing for us. We, too, wish to dance."

"But I have not time. I am in a great hurry," answered the little Rabbit.

"No, no! do not go! Sing for us, — only a little while," cried all the Turkeys.

"Very well, I will sing for you a little while; but you must hasten. Come, all of you, and stand around me," said the little Rabbit.

All the Turkeys came and stood in a circle around the little gray Rabbit. When all were ready the little Rabbit said: "I will sit in the middle and sing. You, who are fat, must pass close to me as you dance. But you must all shut your eyes; if you open them your eyes will be red!" All the Turkeys shut their eyes and began to dance in a circle

DANCING INDIAN

14

around the little Rabbit. As they danced he sang:

> "Alas for him who looks!
>> Eyes will be red; eyes will be red!
> Flirt your tails out widely!"

But as the fat Turkeys went by, the little Rabbit knocked them down and put them into his game bag.

At last a young Turkey grew tired of holding his eyes shut. He opened one eye a little and looked around. The little Rabbit was just putting a fat Turkey into his bag. At once the young Turkey began to scream:

> "Look ye! Look ye!
> The Rabbit is killing us!
> Look ye! look ye!"

At this all the Turkeys opened their eyes and flew away with a great noise.

When the little Rabbit came home he was quite proud of what he had done. He gave the bag of Turkeys to his grandmother and said: "Grandmother, here is a bag full of game. Watch it while I go for some sticks to make spits. But do not open the bag."

The little Rabbit then went out after the spits. While he was gone his grandmother watched the bag of game. But she wished very much to know what was inside.

"Surely it will do no harm to look," she said at last. "I will open the bag only a little bit."

She untied the string about the mouth of the bag. At once the Turkeys burst out, screaming and flapping their great wings.

They knocked the old Rabbit grandmother down on the floor. Then they all flew out through the smoke hole. The old grandmother sprang up but caught only one small Turkey by the legs.

GRAY RABBIT, OR COTTONTAIL

When the little gray Rabbit came home again he was angry.

"Grandmother, I told you not to open the bag! Now we shall have only one small Turkey to eat," he cried.

"It is even so, grandson," she said, weeping.

So the little Rabbit and his grandmother sat down with only one small Turkey between them.

Ever since then, the Indians say, Turkeys have red eyes. This is because they opened their eyes when the little gray Rabbit sang for them.

III

THE SUN MAN AND THE MOON

In his yellow earth lodge,
By the prairie wide,
Lived the golden Sun Man,
With his shining bride.
And his lovely bride wife —
Could you ever guess? —
Was the gentle Moon Squaw,
In her silver dress.

From his yellow earth lodge,
With the morning light,
Came the golden Sun Man,
Shining round and bright;
And the hunters hastened,
Some to chase the deer,
Some to slay the antelope,
Buffalo, or bear.

17

When the falling twilight
Deepened o'er the plain,
And the silver Moon Squaw
Softly shone again,
Home the hunters hastened,
East and north and west,
Rolled them in their bison robes
And lay down to rest.

This the golden Sun Man
Did not like a bit;
Hot he grew and angry
When he thought of it.
"Ho! You wicked Moon Squaw!"
To his wife he cried;
"Do not call my hunters back
From the prairies wide!"

Said the gentle Moon Squaw,
"Do not chase away
All my silver sky stars
With your yellow day!
When the night to slumber
Calls the Indian men,
Do not shine each morning,
And waken them again."

But the angry Sun Man
Hot and hotter grew;
Straight his leather moccasin
At his wife he threw.
"Ho! you wicked Moon Squaw!
I will climb the sky,
O'er the earth, a light for men,
Shining bright and high."

Laughed the silver Moon Squaw:
"Everywhere you go
In the starry sky path
I will follow too.
Though the day shall summon
The hunters to the plain,
I will come with darkness
And call them back again."

Still the golden Sun Man
In the sky is seen;
Every day he summons
The hunters to the plain;
But the silver Moon Squaw
Follows in his path,
Calls the hunters home again,
Laughing at his wrath.

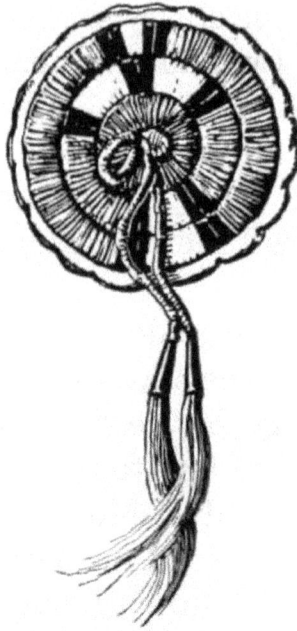

PORCUPINE - QUILLED ROSETTE

BEADED TURTLE AMULET

IV

WUCHOWSON[1] THE WIND BLOWER

An Indian had his wigwam near the sea, at a place where there was good fishing. He often went out in his canoe and speared fish, or caught them in his nets.

When fall came and the geese were flying South, the weather grew windy. A gale arose on the sea, and the waves roared and foamed against the shore. The Indian had never seen it blow so hard in his life.

WILD GEESE

Day after day went by, but still it blew. The wind howled and the waves rolled like mountains.

[1] Wü chow´ sôn

21

Each morning the Indian dragged his canoe down to the water's edge and made ready his nets; but he could neither paddle nor steer his canoe in such a gale. He became quite vexed at last.

"It is Wuchowson the Wind Blower who does this," he said. "He is fanning the wind with his wings. I will ask him not to move his wings so fast. Then the waves will go down and I can spear fish once more."

He put away his nets, took his bow and some pemmican[1], and started off. After many weeks he came to the place in the North where Wuchowson lives.

Here he saw a tall rock rising up at the edge of the sky; On the rock sat Wuchowson. His broad wings were spread like two clouds, and when he swept them through the air the wind howled and roared and rushed out over the sea.

Wuchowson was a great white eagle, taller than a hill. The Indian climbed to the top of the rock where the great eagle sat. He spoke boldly to Wuchowson.

EAGLE

"Ho, Wind Blower!" he said; "do not move your wings so fast.

[1] Pĕm´ mĭ kɑn

22

The wind raises the waves so that I cannot paddle my canoe nor use my nets."

But Wuchowson looked down at the Indian and laughed. He swept his broad wings through the air and the wind roared louder than ever. Then he said: "Go away! I do not care if the wind does blow the waves. Long before men went upon the sea I moved my wings and screamed."

This made the Indian quite angry. His eyes glinted like fire.

"Very well, Wind Blower," he cried; "I will tie your wings so that you cannot move them."

He threw the great eagle down upon his back, tied his wings with ropes, and dragged him to a dark place between two rocks. There the Indian left him and went home.

He was quite happy when he came to his wigwam. He could now go out in his canoe and fish whenever he liked. The wind had died and there was a calm.

FISH SPEAR

But by and by a change came over the sea. The water grew foul and stagnant. A thick white scum spread over all its surface.

Many fishes died and floated upon the water. The Indian could

23

not even go out upon the sea in his canoe. He could not push his paddle through the thick scum.

At last he left his wigwam and set out again for the North. After many weeks he came to the place where Wuchowson lay.

He lifted the great eagle out of the dark place and set him again on the tall rock. Then he loosed one of the Wind Blower's wings. The other wing he left tied as before.

Wuchowson began to move his great wing and the wind blew once more. Soon the thick scum went away from the sea.

But the winds never blow so hard now, for Wuchowson can move only one of his wings.

V

THE LITTLE ICE MAN

An Indian village stood by a deep forest. It was a large village and had a council house. A spring bubbled out of the ground near by, and a tall poplar tree rose in the forest beyond.

Autumn came; the winds blew, and the ground in the forest was covered with leaves. The Indians fetched coals and set fire to the dry leaves to burn out the brush.

But the flames spread and many forest trees were burned. The wind blew sparks and burning leaves into the poplar tree until its branches caught fire. The smoke was thick and black.

The Indians came out and watched the poplar burn. The hot flames roared through the thick tree top. One by one the branches fell, until only the trunk was left. It, too, came down at last with a crash.

The Indians were glad when they saw the trunk fall. They were afraid their village might be set on fire by flying sparks.

"The tree has fallen; now the fire will die," they cried.

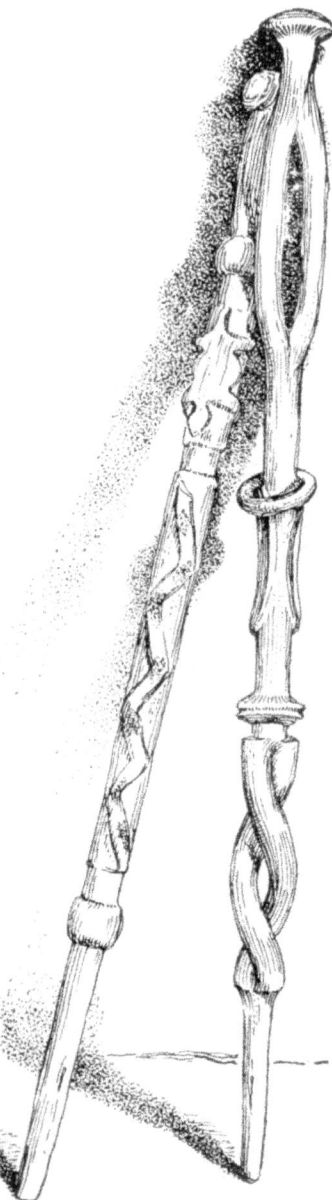

OLD MEN'S WALKING STICKS
(Dakota Indians)

But the fire did not die. The roots of the tree still burned, and the fire went into the ground. A deep pit opened in the place where the trunk had stood. From the pit came flame and hot smoke.

The Indians became frightened. They thought the world was going to burn up.

"Let us pour water on the fire; if the pit grows, the world will burn," they cried.

The women carried water from the spring in kettles and poured it into the pit. Clouds of hot steam arose, but the fire burned on as before.

"Fetch more kettles! Pour on more water!" cried the Indians.

The women ran to the village for more kettles. Young girls brought bowls and clay pots and all poured water into the pit. But the fire burned, hot as ever.

The Indians became more and more frightened. The pit was

growing and the fire was coming close to their village. Their chief called them to a council in the council house.

"What shall we do?" he asked. "If the fire is not put out the world will burn. We shall all die."

He sat down, and there was silence in the council. At last an old man arose at a place near the door. He was old and thin, and had to lean on a stick as he spoke.

"I will tell you what to do," he said. "Go to the little Ice Man. He lives in the North in a wigwam of ice. He will know how to put out the fire."

The Indians had never heard of the Ice Man and his wigwam. Some laughed, thinking the old man was foolish; but their chief said to him: "Grandfather, we will do as you say. We will choose three swift runners. They shall go to the Ice Man and ask him to put out the fire."

So the Indians chose three young men who were swift runners and said to them: "Go to the Ice Man. Tell him of the pit and ask him to put out the big fire."

The three young men put on new moccasins and hastened away.

MOCCASINS

All day and all that night they ran. On the next day they came to

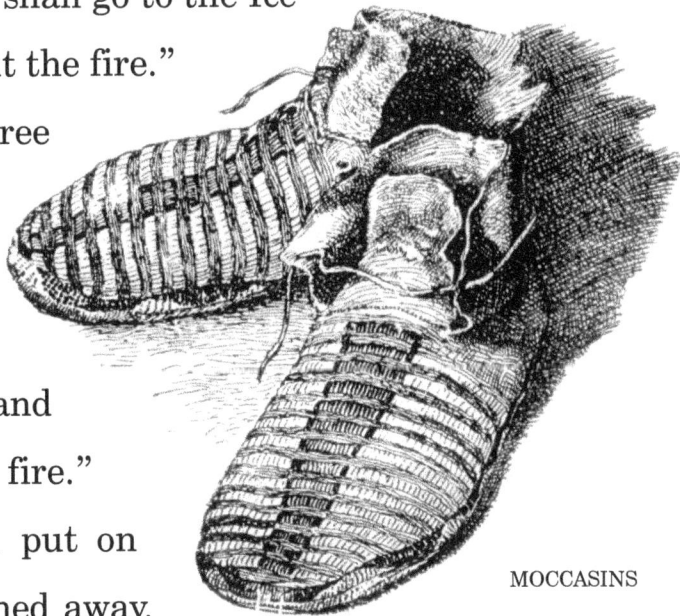

27

the North where the Ice Man lives.

Here they found a great wigwam made of ice. It was roofed like a cabin. A thick bearskin hung over the door.

The young men pushed the bearskin aside and went in. They found the Ice Man sitting on the floor on a mat.

He was a funny-looking little man. His hair hung over his shoulders in two braids. His face was wrinkled and his skin was puckered like old leather. But he had kind eyes.

He looked up, smiling, as the young men entered, and made a place for them by the fire.

"Come and sit on the other side of the fire, away from the door," he said.

They sat down and the Ice Man gave them his pipe to smoke. When they were rested the eldest of the young men spoke.

"Grandfather, near our village is a fire. It is in a pit. Each day the pit grows deeper and we fear the world will burn. We have come to ask you to put out the fire."

For a while the Ice Man did not answer. He took his pipe again and sat on the mat, smoking. At last he laid the pipe down upon the floor.

"I will put out the fire," he said.

As he spoke he began to unplait the braids of his hair. When the ends were loose he took them up in his hand and struck them over his open palm.

At once a cold wind began to blow. It seemed to come from the ends of the loose hair.

The Ice Man struck his palm a second time and rain began to fall.

When he struck his palm the third time sleet fell with the rain. Colder grew the air, and the floor of the wigwam became wet and icy with the sleet.

But the Ice Man had not done. Once more he struck the palm with the loose hair.

The rain now turned to hail; the wind moaned; the walls of the wigwam creaked and groaned; hailstones as big as owls' eggs rolled upon the floor.

The Ice Man looked at the three young men and smiled.

"Go home," he said. "When you come to your village wait for me. You will hear me in the storm."

The young men hastened home and told the villagers what the Ice Man had said. The next day all came out and stood near the burning pit.

In a little while a black cloud came up in the North and overspread the sky. Overhead the wind whistled and moaned. The fire in the pit burned fiercer than ever.

Cold rain and sleet began to fall. The raindrops sputtered as they fell in the hot fire.

Suddenly with the rain there came a fierce storm of hail. The

Indians covered their heads and ran shouting to their wigwams; hailstones as big as owls' eggs were falling from the sky.

Harder and harder fell the hail. The fire in the pit roared and white steam went up in clouds. A whirlwind drove the hailstones into every corner of the burning pit.

At last the storm ceased; the clouds rolled away; the sun shone again and the Indians came out of their wigwams.

In the place where the pit had been there was a wide lake.

The Indians came and stood on the shore of the lake. Deep under the water they heard a sound.

Hiss-s-s it went, as if some one were pouring water on a hot fire.

VI

GLOOSKAP[1] AND THE WINTER GIANT

There once lived a man whose name was Glooskap. He kept two tame wolves about his wigwam. One wolf was white like day; the other was black like night. Glooskap called them his hunting dogs.

He often took them out with him to hunt, when he would say to them, "Dogs, grow big!"

At once the two wolves would grow as big as bears.

When he had done hunting, Glooskap would say, "Dogs, grow small!" and the wolves would become small as before.

WOLF

Glooskap's wigwam stood alone, for he did not like to dwell near other people. His old grandmother cooked for him and mended his moccasins.

[1] Gloos´ käp

One day he came home with a fat deer on his shoulders. He threw the deer on the ground before the door and went into the wigwam. His grandmother was stirring a pot of fat on the fire.

"Here, grandmother," he cried, "I have brought you some meat. I am tired of staying in the wigwam; I am going off on a journey."

He put a knife in his belt, took

CARIBOU, OR NORTHERN DEER

his bow, and went out without saying another word. His grandmother stopped stirring the fat and watched him as he went out of the door.

"My grandson is brave, — he will do something wonderful," she said; and she began to stir the fat again over the fire.

When Glooskap left the wigwam he set off toward the North. It was summer when he started, but after a time the air began to grow colder, the forest leaves turned red and fell to the ground, and the

EARTHEN COOKING POT

rivers froze hard with ice. Glooskap had to put on snowshoes, for the ground had become covered with snow.

He came at last to the far North, where he saw a tall wigwam standing alone in the snow. Snowdrifts were piled about its sides and a white bearskin hung over the door. Glooskap lifted the bearskin and looked in. There sat a great giant inside.

FLINT KNIVES

The giant was old. Deep wrinkles were in his face, and his hair was white like snow. Glooskap wondered who he was.

"Grandfather, who are you?" he asked.

TOBACCO

"I am Winter; I bring the snow and ice," answered the giant.

He then invited Glooskap to come into the wigwam.

Glooskap stooped his head under the bearskin and went in. The giant gave him a seat beside the fire and filled a pipe with sweet tobacco. As they smoked, the giant told wonderful tales of olden times. Glooskap was astonished.

"Wonderful! I never heard such strange stories," he cried.

But as the giant talked a change came over Glooskap. He grew chilled; his head began to nod; his eyes closed; the pipe fell out of his mouth.

TOAD

He rolled over at last and lay on the floor like a fat, sleepy toad. The Winter Giant had charmed him to sleep.

For six months he lay on the giant's floor. The charm then left him and Glooskap awoke. He was angry when he found what the giant had done.

"The Winter Giant has mocked me, but perhaps I shall mock him," he thought.

Then he said aloud to the giant, "Grandfather, I must be going." And he left the wigwam and went away toward the South.

For weeks he journeyed on, until he came to the Summer country, where strange little men were dancing under the trees. They were the Little People of the South. As they danced they shook rattles and sang.

The Summer Woman was their queen. A wee little woman she was, scarcely taller than a

TURTLE - SHELL
RATTLE

34

warrior's foot. All the little men loved her and obeyed her.

Glooskap was glad when he saw the little Summer Woman.

"I will steal her and take her away with me; then I can mock the Winter Giant," he thought.

He went into the forest, killed a moose, and cut its skin into a long string. This he wound into a ball and came again to the place where the little men were dancing.

When her people were not looking, Glooskap caught up the little queen and ran off with her. As he ran he unwound the moose-string ball and let the loose end drag behind him.

The little men were terribly angry. They shouted shrill cries and ran after Glooskap, hoping to catch him. Soon they found the end of the moose-skin string which he had dropped.

"Let us pull at the string! It is tied to Glooskap. Thus we shall stop him," they cried.

So all the little men pulled stoutly at the moose-skin string, thinking they were pulling Glooskap; but they were only un-winding the ball.

Once more Glooskap came to the Winter Giant's wigwam. The giant welcomed him, for he hoped to charm Glooskap again; but this time Glooskap had the little Summer Woman hid under his coat.

As before, he went into the wigwam and sat down. Again the giant gave him a pipe full of sweet tobacco. As they smoked,

Glooskap told wonderful tales to the giant.

By and by a change came over the giant. Sweat ran down his face; his voice grew weak; his legs trembled; water ran out of his eyes.

At last he fell down on the floor and melted away. The wigwam fell in and melted, too. Nothing was left of it but a bare place on the ground.

The snow melted and ran into the rivers. Grass and flowers came out of the ground. Everything was beautiful, for spring had come.

And all the little men came, too. They had followed the moose-skin string which Glooskap had let fall behind him.

Glooskap gave the little Summer Woman back to them, and the little men danced and sang once more.

Then Glooskap went back to his home.

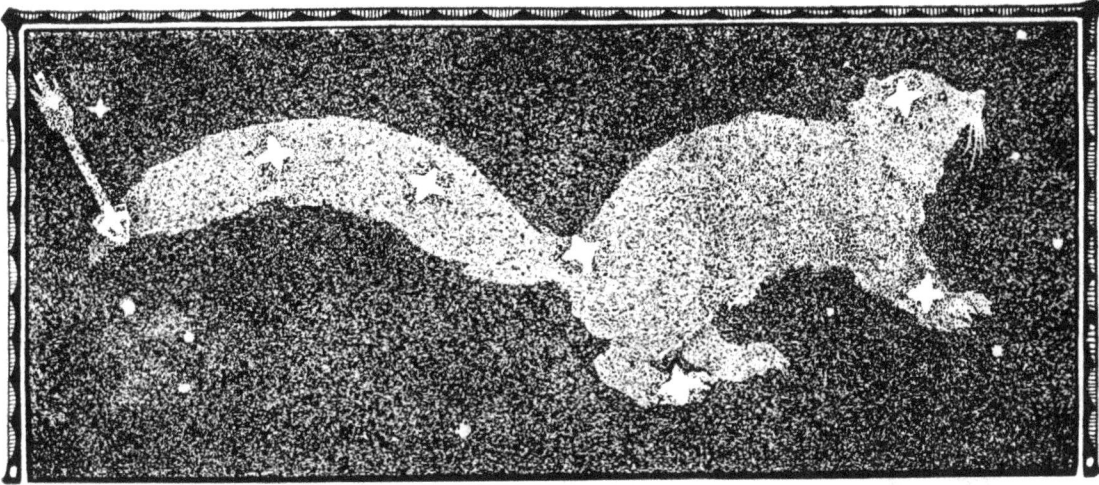

VII

THE FISHER WHO LET OUT SUMMER

I. THE RED SQUIRREL

A Fisher had his wigwam on the shore of a lake. It was a good place for winter camping. There were fish to be caught through the ice, and the waters of the lake were sweet to drink. In the forest near by were many deer.

While her husband hunted, the Fisher's wife watched the fire and cared for their little son. The little boy was just old enough to hunt small game.

One day the little boy's father brought home a bow and a small quiver of arrows.

"Little son," he said, "you must learn how to hunt. Take this bow. In the forest are birds and squirrels. Go and shoot them with your arrows."

The little boy was quite proud to own a bow. Every day, as his father bade him, he went into the forest to hunt birds.

But it was bitter cold in the forest. Deep snow was on the ground, and many of the birds had flown away. Often the little boy came home with his fingers almost frozen.

One evening he came back weeping. He had seen no birds, and he was chilled and cold.

FISHER OR PENNANT'S MARTEN

As he came in sight of the wigwam a red Squirrel ran into his path. The boy raised his bow to shoot.

"Little brother, little brother, do not shoot me!" cried the Squirrel.

The little boy put down his bow. He was surprised to hear the Squirrel speak.

"Little brother," said the Squirrel, "I know why you weep. It is because you are cold and have seen no birds. You must ask your father to let out summer."

"Why should I do that?" said the little boy.

"If summer is here the air will be warm

BOW AND QUIVER

38

and the birds will come again. Nuts will grow on the trees and I shall then have something to eat," answered the Squirrel.

RED, OR PINE, SQUIRREL

The little boy did not know what to think of this. He went home wondering what it could mean.

Before it was dark the Fisher came in from hunting. When the little boy saw his father he began to weep again.

"Little son, what is the matter?" asked the Fisher.

"Father, I am cold, and I have seen no birds. I want you to let out summer. Then the air will be warm and the birds will come again," answered the little boy.

The Fisher sat and thought. He drew a pipe from his pouch and smoked it a long time. At last he spoke: "Little son, do not weep. I will try to let out summer; but it will be no easy thing to do."

II. THE BIG HEAD

The next day the Fisher made a feast in his wigwam and invited five friends. They were the Otter, the Beaver, the Lynx, the Badger, and the Wolverine.

39

The friends came, each bringing a wooden bowl and a spoon. The Fisher's wife had roasted a fat bear, and the feast lasted all day. When evening came the Fisher pushed aside his bowl and said: "My friends, I am going to the sky country to let out summer. Come with me. The journey is long, but you are brave and will not fear to go."

The friends thought for a while before they answered. Then the Otter spoke: "We will go. We are not afraid."

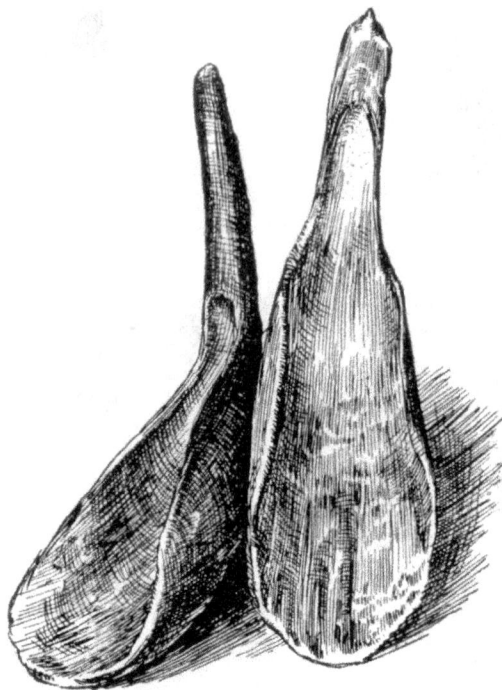

BUFFALO - HORN SPOONS

They started the next morning. The Fisher led; the others followed, stepping in his tracks. For days they went on, hardly stopping to eat or sleep. On the twentieth day they came to the foot of a high mountain.

Here they found tracks of moccasins in the snow. The hard crust was trampled down and blood lay on the ground, as if some one had killed a deer.

The friends stopped. They had no wish to climb the mountain, for evening was already near. None of them knew which way to go.

"Let us follow the tracks," said the Fisher at last.

He started off as the tracks led, and the others followed. They soon came to a bark wigwam hidden in a hollow.

As they drew near, a queer-looking man came to the door. He was like a big, ugly head, with neither arms nor hands. Crooked teeth stood in his mouth and he had fierce eyes. But he spoke kindly to the friends.

"Come into my wigwam," he said. "I will cook you some meat, and you can sleep tonight on my bearskins."

They went in, and the Big Head fetched from a corner a large wooden bowl. He put in some meat and set the bowl on the fire like a kettle. The fire did it no harm.

When the meat had boiled, the Big Head took the bowl from the fire and set it before the friends. They wondered to see him do this without arms or hands. He moved so quickly that they did not see how he lifted the bowl.

But he looked queer, stumping about on his short legs.

OTTER

His big, ugly face made so many odd motions that the Otter could not keep from laughing. This angered the Big Head.

"You wicked Otter, how dare you laugh at me!" he screamed. And he sprang on the Otter's neck to strangle him.

Over they rolled, fighting and struggling fiercely. It was well for

the Otter that his fur was sleek. Stretching his long body, he wriggled out between the Big Head's legs and ran out of the door into the night.

The Fisher and his four friends stayed all night in the wigwam. Early the next morning they made ready to go. The Big Head then said to them: "I know you are going to the sky country to let out summer. Do not fear. Journey for twenty days more, until you come to the top of a high mountain. You will then be near the sky."

The friends thanked him and went on. A little way from the wigwam they found the Otter. He had slept in the snow and was nigh dead with hunger.

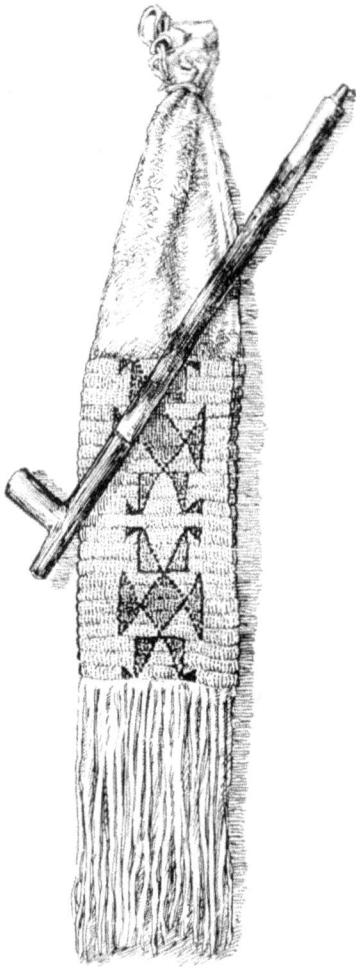

PIPE AND TOBACCO POUCH

The Fisher had some of the meat which the Big Head had given him. This he gave to the Otter and all went on through the snow.

III. THE SKY COUNTRY

On the twentieth day they came again to a high mountain, and reached the top after a hard climb. Here they rested awhile. The Fisher drew his pipe from its pouch and gave it to his friends to smoke. At last he arose.

"Who will break a hole in the sky?" he asked.

"I will," cried the Otter; "I know how to jump."

He stood, bent his lithe body, and leaped. High up he went, like a black arrow; but

BEAVER

he did not reach the sky. In a moment he fell back, and rolled down the side of the mountain stunned. When he opened his eyes his head swam and he was aching in every bone.

"Let others break the sky; I have enough!" he cried, as he limped home over the snow.

LYNX

The Fisher and his four friends were still on the top of the mountain.

"Let me try to break the sky," said the Beaver.

He bent his back like a great bow and leaped upward; but he went only a little higher than the Otter had gone.

Then the Lynx and the Badger tried. They, too, could not reach the sky. Only the Wolverine was left.

"Let me try; my father taught me how to jump," he cried.

BADGER

He humped his back, put his nose in the air, and leaped. High overhead he went, until he looked like a black speck among the clouds. In a little while he fell back; but he had touched the sky with his head.

Again he leaped. This time he struck the sky and cracked it. When he leaped the third time he passed through, breaking a great hole.

The Fisher then leaped up after him, and the two friends found themselves in the sky country. It was a good land. There were mountains and rivers and bright grasses. The white sun shone overhead and the air was warm and sweet. Everywhere was the soft, beautiful summer.

A little way off stood a village of wigwams. Thither the two friends now made their way. They found the villagers gone, but in the wigwams hung wooden cages full of many kinds of birds. The Fisher thought of his little son.

"If I break the cages the birds will fly down to earth," he said.

All this time the warm air was pouring out of the sky. It made a loud noise as it rushed through the great hole. This alarmed the villagers. They all came running home to see what it was that made the noise.

The Wolverine saw them coming and leaped through the hole to the top of the mountain again. The Fisher stayed to let out the birds.

At last all the cages were broken and he, too, ran to the big hole. But the villagers had closed it; they did not want the warm air to quit the sky, for they feared winter would then come into the sky country.

That, too, is why we have summer only part of the year. Had no one

WOLVERINE

closed the hole, all the warm air would have left the sky and we should have summer every month.

The villagers were fiercely angered when they saw the Fisher.

"There he is—he who broke our sky! Kill him! kill him!" they cried. And they began to shoot at him with their arrows.

He fled far to the North. Near the end of the sky he climbed a tree and tried to hide in its thick branches. The villagers came below and shot upward through the tree top. Toward evening one of them wounded the Fisher in the tail. Then they left him.

Night had come, and all was still, when the Fisher climbed down from the tree. He was faint and bleeding. He crept a little way, staggered and fell upon his side.

"I am dying," he whispered; "but my little son will be happy. I have let out summer. Now the snow will go, and birds will come again into the forest."

In the morning the villagers found him lying on the sky. He was dead.

"Let him lie," they said; "he shall be a warning to men. Then they will not try again to come into our sky."

When the night is bright the Fisher may still be seen among the stars. The arrow is sticking in his tail.

VIII

THE RAINBOW SNAKE

Have you heard of the beautiful Rainbow Snake
Whose scales move to and fro,
As he arches his back to the blue sky floor,
And scratches off rain and snow?

Away in the West, where the Indians dwell,
In the land of the buffalo,
They tell this tale of the Rainbow Snake
Who sends down rain and snow.

Long, long ago, ere the white man came,
The rivers and lakes ran low,
And the brooks dried up, and the fishes died,
And the elk and the buffalo.

And the Indians cried, "Alas, we die!
No longer the rose pods grow;
And the rivers and brooks and ponds are dry,
For there falls no rain nor snow."

Then a little Snake wriggled him out of the grass
And said, "My brothers, I know
That if I can only climb up to the sky,
I can send down rain and snow.

"For of blue, blue ice is the blue sky floor,
And it maketh the cold winds blow;
And if I can only climb up to the ice,
I can scrape down rain and snow."

So the little Snake stretched and stretched himself,
And made himself grow and grow,
Until he was long as a river is long
Whose waters to ocean flow.

And he climbed the clouds to the cold ice sky,
Where his tail and his head drop low,
As he arches his back to the blue sky floor
And scratches off rain and snow.

For he wriggles, and wriggles, and wriggles himself,

And his scales move to and fro,

And scrape the ice sky in the winter time,

And then we have beautiful snow.

But when in the summer he wriggles himself,

And the clouds roll over the plain,

The ice flakes melt as they fall to earth,

And then we have beautiful rain.

And still in the sky is the Rainbow Snake,

The serpent of long ago;

And he wriggles, and wriggles, and wriggles himself,

And scratches off rain and snow.

IX

LITTLE SCAR FACE

In a village by a lake dwelt a young warrior named Team.[1] He had no kinsfolk except a sister who kept house for him. She was called the White Maiden.

No one had ever seen Team. The villagers could hear his footsteps as he went by, and they could see his tracks in the snow, but Team himself they never saw; he was invisible.

One day Team's sister called the village maidens to the council house. When all were come in and sat in a great circle in the council room she said to them: "My brother Team wishes to marry. He is a young man and very rich, but he is invisible; no one can see him who is not gentle and good. Therefore, if any maiden can see him, he will have her for his wife."

[1] Tēαm.

50

The village maidens were all joyful when they heard this. They knew Team was young and rich. In her heart each hoped to have him for her husband.

Every evening, then, as the sun set, some of the maidens would go down by the lake to Team's wigwam. The White Maiden always invited them to come in, and they would sit and watch by the wigwam fire.

By and by, as they sat, they would hear footsteps. Then the door flap would open and some one would enter. But the maidens could never see any one.

At the other end of the village, near the bushes, lived an old man with his three daughters. The two elder daughters were young women, but the youngest was only a girl.

The elder sisters were very unkind to the little girl. They made her do all the work and gave her only bones and scraps to eat.

But the eldest was the more unkind. Often, when she was angry, she would throw ashes and hot coals in her sister's face. In this way the little girl's hair was burned and her face became marked and scarred. So the villagers named her little Scar Face.

Her father never knew how unkind her elder sisters were. In the evening, when he came home from his hunt, he would sometimes say to the little girl, "Why is it that your face is always scarred and burned?"

And before little Scar Face could answer her eldest sister would say: "Father, it is because she goes near the fire and falls in. We tell her not to go there, but she will not obey us."

One day in winter, when the first snow lay on the ground, the eldest sister said: "Little Scar Face, bring me my shell beads and my moccasins. I am going to marry Team!"

Little Scar Face brought the beads and the moccasins and helped her sister put them on.

In the evening, as the sun set, the eldest sister went down by the lake to Team's wigwam. The White Maiden invited her to come inside.

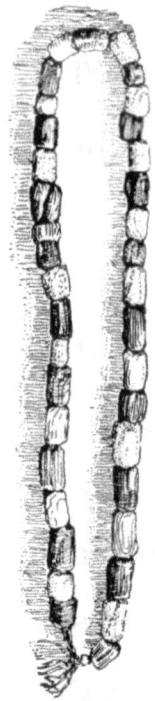

SHELL BEADS

MOOSE

By and by they heard footsteps. Outside the wigwam there was a sound as if some one was dragging a sledge through the snow. The White Maiden led little Scar Face's sister to the door and said to her, "Can you see my brother?"

"Yes, I can see him very well," she answered.

"Then tell me, of what is his sledge string made?" said the White Maiden.

And the other answered, "It is made of moose skin."

52

This made the White Maiden angry.

"No, it is not made of moose skin! You have not seen my brother. You must go away," she cried. And she drove little Scar Face's sister out of the wigwam.

The next day little Scar Face's second sister said to her: "Little Scar Face, bring me my shell beads and my moccasins. I am going to marry Team!"

Little Scar Face brought the beads and the moccasins and her sister put them on.

In the evening, then, as the sun was setting, the second sister went down to Team's wigwam. The White Maiden invited her to come in.

INDIAN SLEDGE, OR TOBOGGAN

By and by she, too, heard footsteps. Then the White Maiden said to her, "Can you see my brother?"

"Yes, I can see him very well," she answered.

"Of what is his sledge string made?" asked the White Maiden.

And the other answered, "It is made of deerskin."

At this the White Maiden became angry again.

"No, it is not made of deerskin! You have not seen my brother.

INDIAN WOOD PILE

"You, too, must go away," she cried. And she drove the second sister out of the wigwam.

The next morning, while her two sisters sat and talked, little Scar Face worked very hard. She scoured the kettle and carried out the ashes and fetched a great pile of wood for the fire. Then she said to her two sisters: "Elder sisters, lend me your shell beads and your moccasins. I, too, should like to try to marry Team."

But her sisters laughed and mocked at the little girl. They would not lend her any moccasins. At last her second sister gave her some strings of beads that were very small.

In a corner of the wigwam far from the door little Scar Face found a pair of old moccasins that her father had thrown away. They were dry and hard and were too big for her. She soaked them in water to make them soft.

She had no pretty clothing to wear, but she made herself a queer little dress out of birch bark.

She looked very ugly with her scarred face and short hair. As she went through the village the dogs barked at her and the people laughed and called out,

"Oho! look at little Scar Face!
Oho! look at little Scar Face!"

But when she came to Team's wigwam the White Maiden spoke kindly to her.

"Come into the wigwam, little Scar Face," she said.

Little Scar Face went in and sat down. By and by she heard footsteps. Then the White Maiden led her to the door and said, "Little Scar Face, can you see my brother?"

INDIAN DOG

"Yes, I can see him; and I am afraid, for he is wonderful," answered little Scar Face.

"Then tell me, of what is his sledge string made?" said the White Maiden.

"How wonderful! His sledge string is the rainbow," cried little Scar Face.

When Team heard this he smiled and said to his sister, "Elder sister, bathe little Scar Face's hair and eyes in the magic water."

And when she did so a wonderful thing happened. All the scars and burns faded away from the little girl's face. Her hair came out long and black. Her eyes were like two round stars.

The White Maiden then led her to the wife's seat beside the door.

Thus little Scar Face saw Team, and he had her for his wife.

X

HOW THE LITTLE RABBIT SNARED
THE SUN

Once the little Rabbit and his grandmother moved their tent to new hunting grounds. Summer had gone and the trees in the woodland were turning yellow. It was time for the little Rabbit to lay in meat for winter.

Each morning he awoke early, took his bow and quiver, and went out to hunt. In the evening he came back with meat and skins. His grandmother dried the meat and made the skins into robes for winter.

One evening the little Rabbit came home walking very fast. He threw down a pack of skins before the door and went into the tent. He was quite vexed.

"Grandmother," he cried, "each morning I awake early and go to the woodland to hunt, but some one is always there before me; and he has a very long foot, — I can see his tracks in the path."

"Grandson, you must get up earlier," said his grandmother.

The next morning the little Rabbit awoke very early. He put on his moccasins, took his bow and quiver, and went again to hunt; but when he came to the woodland there were the tracks in the path as before.

This greatly vexed the little Rabbit. He could not think who it was that made the tracks. In the evening, when he came home, he said: "Grandmother, I awoke early, but when I came to the path in the woodland some one with a very long foot was before me."

"Grandson, you must get up earlier," said his grandmother.

The next morning the little Rabbit was up before it was day, but when he came to the woodland there were the tracks in the path as

RABBIT SNARE

before. In the evening he said again to his grandmother: "Grandmother, I arose very early, but when I came to the woodland some one was there before me; and he has a very long foot. I should like to know who he is."

"Grandson, you must get up still earlier," said his grandmother.

"No, grandmother; but I will make a snare and catch him," said the little Rabbit.

His grandmother did not want him to do this. She was afraid the little Rabbit might get into trouble.

58

"O grandson, do not do that!" she cried; "you may catch something terrible in your snare."

But the little Rabbit was now angry. He did not like to be beaten at anything.

"Grandmother, I hate him because he gets ahead of me; and he has a very long foot. I am going to catch him," he answered.

So the little Rabbit sat down in the tent and made a snare out of his bowstring. He then went to the woodland where he had seen the tracks. He put the snare in the middle of the path.

Early the next morning he went to the place where the snare was set. As he drew near he saw that the woodland was light like midday.

The little Rabbit wondered at this; but when he came in sight of the path he was astonished. He found that he had caught the Sun in his snare.

This frightened the little Rabbit. He turned and ran home again as fast as he could run. He found his grandmother bringing in some wood for the fire. She had just raised the door flap to go into the tent.

The little Rabbit stopped when he saw his grandmother. His heart was beating and his breath came very fast.

INDIAN WOMAN BRINGING
IN WOOD

59

"O grandmother," he cried, "I have caught something bright in my snare! I am afraid to go near it. It scares me dreadfully."

His grandmother let fall the load of wood that was on her back. She was more frightened, even, than the little Rabbit.

"O grandson," she cried, "I told you not to set the snare! Now you have caught the Sun. Go at once and cut him loose. If you do

DRYING MEAT

not, he will set fire to the world and burn us up." And she drew her robe over her face and wailed loudly.

"Grandmother, I want to cut the Sun loose, for I should like to get my bowstring again; but every time I go near, the heat scares me," answered the little Rabbit.

But he took his knife and ran back to the place where the Sun was caught. This time he went nearer. When the Sun saw him he cried out: "You very bad Rabbit, why did you catch me? Come here at once and loose me!"

The little Rabbit tried hard to be brave. He took his knife in his hand and ran toward the snare; but the heat was so great that it made him afraid, and he turned again to one side.

All this time the Sun was getting hotter and hotter. He was terribly angry.

"You very bad Rabbit," he cried, "if you do not loose me I will set fire to the world and burn you up!"

The little Rabbit took his knife in his hand once more. He bent down his head and ran toward the Sun with his arm held straight out before him. When he came near he cut the snare and the Sun leaped up into the sky again.

But the Sun was very, very hot. When the little Rabbit stooped to cut the snare, the fur on his back was scorched all yellow with the Sun's heat.

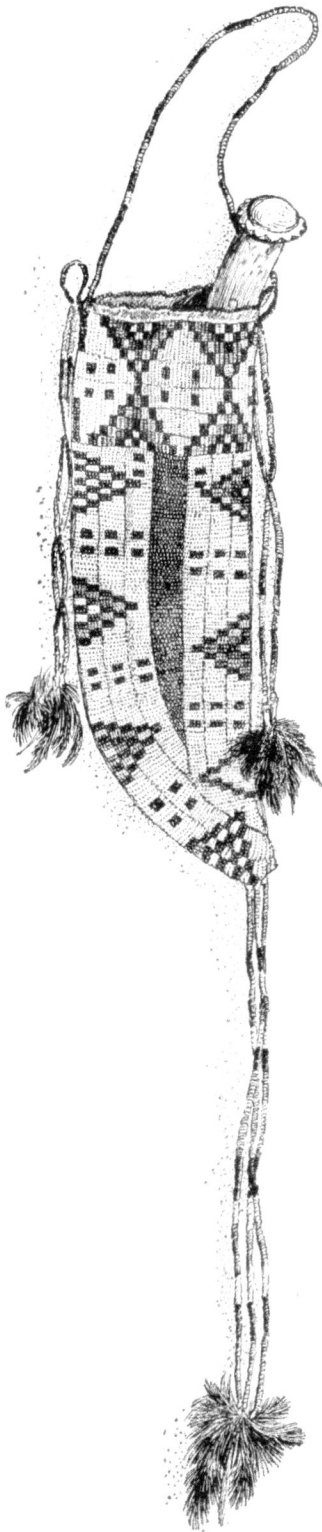

KNIFE WITH BEADED
SHEATH

61

The little Rabbit put his knife back into its sheath and went limping home. He was in great pain.

"O grandmother," he cried, "my back hurts me dreadfully! The Sun has burned my skin and scorched the fur on my back all yellow."

"Grandson," she answered, "I told you not to set the snare. I knew the Sun was hot. That is why I was afraid when he was caught!" But she took the little Rabbit into the tent and spread a robe for him to lie upon.

Ever since that time the little Rabbit has had yellow fur on his back where he was scorched by the Sun's heat.

XI

THE MAGIC WIGWAM

An Indian was walking in the forest when he heard dancing a long way off. He stopped and listened. It was in autumn, when the ground is dry, and he could hear the feet of the dancers beating the ground.

"That is strange," thought the Indian.

"Who can be dancing in the forest to-day?"

He set off toward the sound, to see who the dancers were; but he went for a whole week before he saw any one.

He came at last to two queer old people — an old man and an old woman — dancing around a tree. On a limb in the top of the tree lay a fat raccoon.

The old people had danced until they had worn a deep ditch around the tree. Every time they danced around they made the

63

RACCOON

ditch deeper.

The Indian was much surprised to see the two old people.

"What are you doing?" he asked.

"We are dancing the tree down. When the ditch is deep the tree will fall. Then we will kill the big raccoon and eat his meat," answered the old man.

The Indian laughed and drew a hatchet from his belt. It was made of stone and had a sharp edge.

"That is no way to fell a tree. Let me cut it down for you," he said.

The old man agreed, and the Indian cut down the tree with his

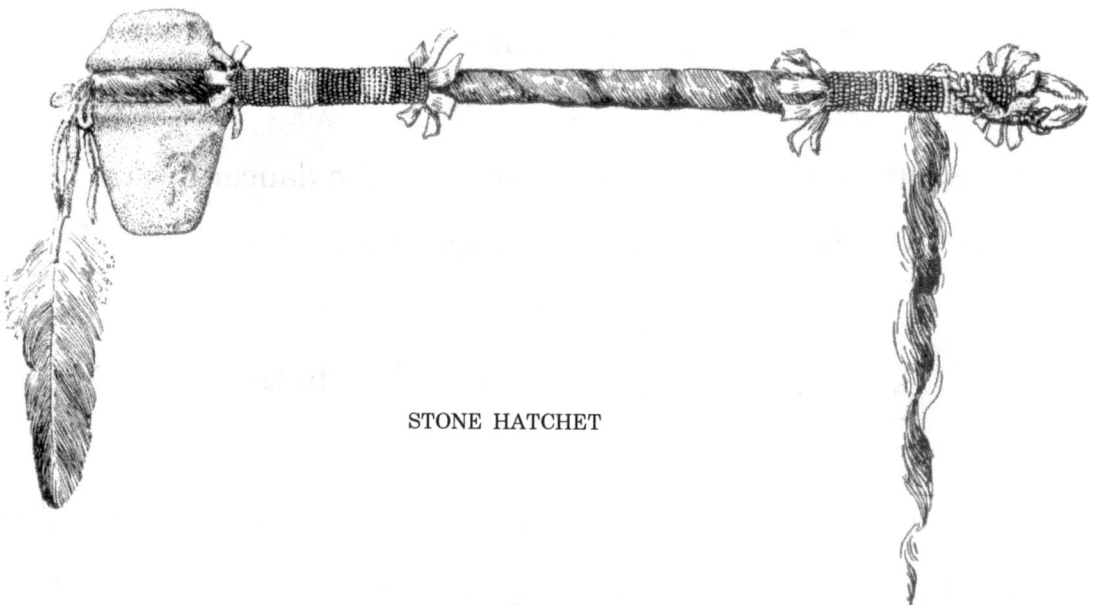

STONE HATCHET

hatchet. They killed the raccoon, and the old woman tanned its skin and gave it to the Indian.

"Grandson," she said, "take this raccoon skin. It is no common pelt. It will bring you luck."

The Indian thanked the two old people, stuck the raccoon skin in his belt, and went on his way.

He had not gone far when he saw something strange through the trees. A man was coming up the path with a birch-bark wigwam on his head. The wigwam was new, and its bark sides shone white like snow.

The Indian felt afraid at first. He thought the man must be one of the magic people.

The stranger put the wigwam on the ground and looked at the Indian. Then he spoke.

"That is a fine skin you have in your belt. Where did you get it?"

"Two queer old people gave it to me. They said it would bring me luck," answered the Indian.

When the stranger heard this he wanted very much to own the raccoon skin.

"I should like to have you sell me the skin," he said.

"What will you give me for it?" asked the Indian.

"I will give you this knife," answered the stranger.

"No; that is not enough," said the other.

"I will give you my bow and arrows," said the stranger.

"No," said the Indian; "that is still too little."

"Then I will give you this beautiful bark wigwam," said the stranger.

The Indian looked at the wigwam. Through the door he saw robes and mats and skins.

"It is a fine wigwam, but it is so large. How shall I be able to carry it?" he asked.

"That is easy," answered the stranger. "The wigwam is light; it is magic."

The Indian lifted the wigwam to his head. Although so large, it was light, like a basket.

"How wonderful! the wigwam is not heavy," he said. He then gave the raccoon skin to the stranger and went on, with the wigwam on his head.

In the afternoon he came to a place where a spring of clear water came out of the ground.

WHITE OR ARCTIC BEAR

"This is a fine place for a camp," he thought. "I will pitch my wigwam here for the winter."

He set the wigwam on the ground and went inside. The sun was setting and the air was getting chilly. The Indian made a fire under the smoke hole and sat down to warm himself.

He was tired, for he had walked a long way. Near the fireplace lay a white bearskin. The Indian drew it toward him and lay down upon it. Soon he fell asleep.

When he awoke the warm sun was shining. He opened his eyes and looked up. He was surprised to see good things to eat hanging from the roof poles.

INDIAN BASKET

There were deer hams and packs of dried meat. Baskets of dried berries and of maple sugar hung there, and many ears of corn.

This made the Indian glad, for he had slept a long time and was hungry. He reached out his arms and sprang upward, hoping to seize the baskets; but a wonderful thing then happened.

His arms became wings. The white bearskin melted and ran away. The roof poles became branches of a birch tree. The deer hams and the

PARTRIDGE, OR ROUGHED GROUSE

baskets of dried berries were turned into birch buds.

He was an Indian no longer, — he was Pulowech[1] the Partridge. He put out his wings and flew into the birch tree, crying gladly, for spring had come.

The white bearskin had been the winter's snow. The wigwam was a snowdrift in which the Partridge had hidden all winter long.

[1] Pŭ′ lō wĕch.

XII

WHY THE BABY SAYS "GOO"

In a village near the mountains lived an Indian chief. He was a brave man and had fought in many battles. No one in the tribe had slain more enemies than he.

Strange folk were then in the land. Fierce ice giants came out of the North and carried away women and children. Wicked witches dwelt in caves, and in the mountains lived the Mikumwess,[1] or magic little people.

But the chief feared none of them. He fought the ice giants and made them go back to their home in the North. Some of the witches he killed; others he drove from the land.

Everybody loved the chief. He was so brave and good that the villagers thought there was no one like him anywhere.

But when he had driven out all the giants the chief grew vain. He

[1] Mīk′ ŭm - wĕss.

69

began to think himself the greatest warrior in the world.

"I can conquer any one," he boasted.

Now it happened that a wise old woman lived in the village. When she heard what the great chief boasted, she smiled.

"Our chief *is* wonderful; but there is one who is mightier than he," she said.

The villagers told the chief what the wise woman had said. He came and visited her in her wigwam.

"Grandmother, who is this wonderful one?" he asked.

"His name is Wasis,"[1] answered the wise woman.

"And where is he, grandmother?" asked the chief.

"He is there," said the wise woman; and she pointed to a place in the wigwam.

The chief looked, — and who do you think Wasis was? He was a plump little Indian Baby. In the middle of the floor he sat, crowing to himself and sucking a piece of maple sugar. He looked very sweet and contended.

Now the chief had no wife, and knew nothing about babies; but he thought, like all vain people, that he knew everything. He thought, of course, that the little Baby would obey him; so he smiled and said to little Wasis:

"Baby, come to me!"

But the baby smiled back and went on sucking his maple sugar.

The chief was surprised. The villagers always did whatever he bade them. He could not understand why the little Baby did not obey him;

[1] Wä′ sĭs

70

but he smiled and said again to little Wasis:

"Baby, come to me!"

The little Baby smiled back and sucked his maple sugar as before.

The chief was astonished. No one had ever dared disobey him before. He grew angry. He frowned at little Wasis and roared out:

"BABY, COME TO ME!"

But little Wasis opened his mouth and burst out crying and screaming. The chief had never heard such awful sounds. Even the ice giants did not scream so terribly.

The chief was more and more astonished. He could not think why such a little Baby would not obey him.

"Wonderful!" he said. "All other men fear me; but this little Baby shouts back war cries. Perhaps I can overcome him with my magic."

He took out his medicine bag and shook it at the little Baby. He danced magic dances. He sang wonderful songs.

Little Wasis smiled and watched the chief with big round eyes. He thought it all very funny. And all the time he sucked his maple sugar.

The chief danced until he was tired out; sweat

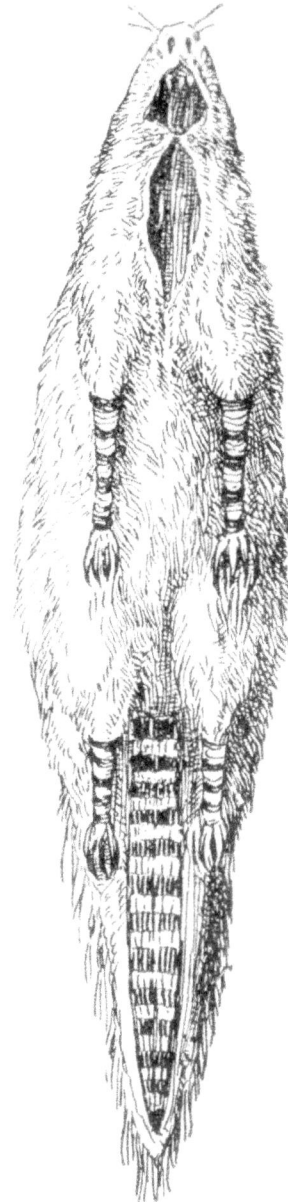

MEDICINE BAG

71

ran down his face; red paint oozed over his cheeks and neck; the feathers in his scalp lock had fallen down.

At last he sat down. He was too tired to dance any longer.

"Did I not tell you that Wasis is mightier than you?" said the wise old woman. "No one is mightier than the Baby. He always rules the wigwam. Everybody loves him and obeys him."

"It is even so," sighed the chief, as he went out of the wigwam.

INDIAN WITH PAINTED FACE

But as he went he could hear little Wasis talking to himself on the floor.

"Goo, goo, goo!" he crowed, as he sucked his maple sugar.

Now, when you hear the Baby saying, "Goo, goo, goo," you will know what it means. It is his war cry. He is happy because he remembers the time when he frightened the chief in the wigwam of the wise old woman.

XIII

THE WREN

The little Wren with speckled coat,

And sweet and cheery cry,

Is the dearest bird in all the wood,

And I will tell you why.

When a baby comes to the Indian's hut

The Wren chirrups for joy,

And hops about on the edge of the roof

And sings, "Is it girl or boy?"

Then to the wood he flies away

To call the birds together, —

Big birds, little birds, pretty and plain,

Birds all, of every feather.

And if he chirrups, "It is a girl,"

The birds sing, joyfully,

"We'll eat the kernels of corn that fall

When she pounds hominy."

But if he chirrups, "It is a boy,"

Loud mourns the feathered choir:

"Alas! alas! He will shoot us with arrows

And fry our shins in the fire!"

XIV

THE GOOD GIANTS

An Indian had his wigwam by the shore of the sea. He was poor and he had many children. Each day he took his canoe and went out upon the sea to fish. His wife often went with him to help him with the nets.

One day when they were fishing a fog arose so that they lost their way. They paddled in every direction, but they could not come to land.

At last, when they were tired and almost ready to give up, they heard voices in the fog. They steered in the direction of the sound and came to a big canoe filled with giants. The giants were young men and their faces were dark like soot. They carried paddles made out of whole trees.

BONE FISH - HOOKS

The Indian and his wife were greatly frightened when they saw the big canoe; but the giants burst out laughing at finding such little folk.

"Ho, little people! where are you going?" they asked.

"We do not know. We have lost our way," answered the Indian.

The giants laughed harder than ever at this.

"Oho! he says he has lost his way!" they roared.

At last they stopped laughing.

"Come with us, little people, and we will take you home to our father," they said.

Two of the giants pushed the ends of their paddles under the Indians' canoe. In this way they lifted it, with the two Indians, into their own.

The giants then steered their canoe to the shore. They did not seem to mind the fog. They paddled straight ahead as if they could see right through it.

On the shore stood three wigwams. They were made of bark and were as tall as mountains.

One of the giants lifted the two Indians in his hand and carried them into the tallest wigwam. Their canoe he hung up on the roof above the door.

Inside the wigwam was an old giant sitting by the fire. He was much surprised when he saw the two Indians.

"Ho, my son! what have you here?" he asked.

"Father, they are two little people that we found in a canoe. They have lost their way in a fog," answered one of the young giants.

The old giant was greatly pleased with his little guests. He called his wife to come and see them.

"But our little people must be hungry," he said at last. "Let us get them something to eat."

His wife brought a wooden bowl and went to a great pot that hung over the fire. She took out a whole whale, hot and steaming, and put it into the bowl. This she set down before the two Indians.

"There, little people," she said, "now you can eat."

WOODEN BOWL

The giants made a place in a corner of the wigwam for the Indians to sleep. They became very fond of their little guests and were never tired of being kind to them.

One morning the old giant came into the wigwam looking troubled.

"Little people," he said, "I have something to tell you. In the North lives a terrible Chenoo,[1] or ice giant. He is our enemy. He

[1] Chĕ′ nū

77

hates us because we are kind to men. In three days he will come to fight us. You must take care that you do not hear his scream. It is terrible. No one can hear it and live."

He told the Indians to stop their ears and wrap themselves in bearskins. In this way they would not hear the ice giant's scream.

In three days the Chenoo came, just as the old giant had said. There was a dreadful battle. Although their ears were stopped, the Indians could hear the ice giant's scream, faintly, through the thick skins. It was terrible.

In a little while the Chenoo screamed a second time. This time his voice did not seem so dreadful. After the third time the old giant came and unwrapped the bearskins.

"Now, little people, you may come out," he said. "The Chenoo is dead. My son killed him with a stone."

But the good giants had suffered too. Their faces and hands were bruised and their legs were stuck full of pine trees, like thistles. Indeed, when they came back to the wigwam one of the young giants fell dead before the door.

But this did not seem to trouble the old giant. He only said, "My son, why are you lying there?"

"Father, it is because I am dead; the Chenoo has killed me," answered the dead giant.

"If that is all, get up at once!" said the old giant.

His son opened his eyes and sat up. He did not seem a bit the worse for having been dead.

Months went by and summer had almost gone. The Indian and his wife began to think of their children far away in the wigwam by the sea. One day the old giant asked them if they wished to go home.

"Yes, for we long to see our children," answered the Indian.

The next morning the old giant took down the Indian's canoe from its place on the roof and put it on the sea. The giant's wife loaded it with furs and packs of dried meat. The canoe sank almost to the water.

When the Indian and his wife had got in, the old giant gave them a little gray dog. He told them to paddle in the direction the little dog pointed. Then he said to the little dog, "Take these people home to their wigwam."

The little dog ran to the middle of the canoe and stood with his paws resting on the edge. He barked and pointed with his nose straight out to sea.

The Indians steered their canoe as the little dog pointed. In a few hours they reached their home. As they came to shore their children ran out to meet them.

The little dog leaped out of the canoe, barking and wagging his tail. He jumped about upon the sand and rubbed his nose into the children's faces. Then he trotted home again over the ocean. He ran over the top of the water just as if it were ice.

After this, whenever the Indian set his nets they came up bursting with fish. If he went hunting he always killed many deer. He grew rich. No one in all the land had more meat and skins than he.

Thus he knew that the good giants had not forgotten him.

XV

THE LITTLE FAWN

A Doe was grazing in an open place in a thicket. With her was her little Fawn who was not yet old enough to eat grass. He skipped about and played among the bushes while his mother fed. At last he ran out to the edge of a meadow that lay beyond.

The little Fawn raised his nose to sniff the sweet air. The wind brought something strange to his smell. Far off over the meadow he saw some black things moving in the grass. They were Indian hunters. They were so far away that they looked like little black specks in the meadow.

The little Fawn was frightened. He put his tail in the air and ran back into the thicket again.

"O mother," he cried; "I see some black things far off in the meadow. They are hiding in the grass. I fear they are men!"

His mother stopped eating for a moment and raised her head.

"No, little son," she said; "they are not men that you see. They are crows. They are feeding in the grass."

But the little Fawn could not rest. Again he ran to the edge of the thicket and looked out. There were the hunters hiding in the grass as before. They were creeping nearer.

The little Fawn ran back to his mother more frightened than ever. His tail stood straight up over his back as he ran.

"Mother," he cried; "the black things are nearer! They are coming toward us! They are creeping through the grass! I know they are men!"

His mother only smiled. "Little son, do not be afraid," she said. "They are not men that you see. They are crows."

CROW

Still the little Fawn could not rest. Once more he ran to the edge of the thicket and looked. This time the hunters were quite near.

The little Fawn was dreadfully frightened and ran again to his mother in the thicket. He ran so fast that his tail bobbed up and down in the air.

"O mother," he cried; "the black things are not crows! They are men; they have bows and arrows; they are very near."

But his mother would not even look up from her feeding.

"No, little son; what you see are only some crows," she said.

Just then the hunters rose up out of the grass. They had arrows on their bowstrings, ready to shoot.

The Doe whistled and leaped away, but the hunters shot her with their arrows. The little Fawn escaped into the bushes.

In the evening the little Fawn crept back to the edge of the thicket. He looked out and saw his mother lying on the ground dead. The hunters had made a fire and were cooking the Doe's liver upon the coals.

INDIAN ARROWS

This made the little Fawn very sad. His head dropped and bright tears stood in his eyes. He turned and crept into the thicket, weeping. He knew he should never see his mother again.

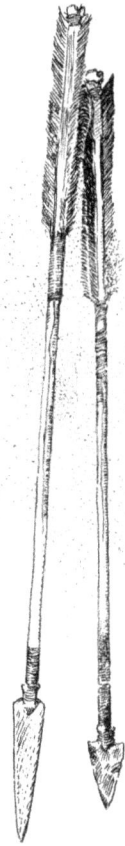

XVI

THE TURKEY MAIDEN

In Salt village, long ago, were many rich families who owned flocks of tame Turkeys.

The Turkeys were kept in wooden cages at night. In the day they had to be driven to the field to feed. Poor people often did this to earn a living.

At the farther end of the village, on the side nearest the field, lived an Indian maiden. Her house had but one room and was old and ugly. Its sides were crumbling and the roof leaked whenever it rained.

The little maiden was alone in the world. Her father had died and she had no brothers to care for her. Her blanket was ragged and her moccasins were full of holes. Her face, too, was thin and pinched, for she was often hungry. Only her eyes were soft and beautiful.

She would have starved if a rich family had not let her care for their Turkeys. For this they gave her scraps of meal cake or a little meat. Sometimes they gave her a piece of worn-out clothing to put on.

No one loved the little maiden, and she was lonely and unhappy. But she was kind to her Turkeys; they were all the friends that she had.

ZUÑI HOUSES

Now it happened that the villagers were going to give a feast and dance. One morning, as the little maiden drove her Turkeys to the field, a crier came out to name the feast day. He stood on a house top and called aloud: "Ho, you people of Salt village! In four days will be the dance of the Sacred Bird."

The little maiden sighed. She had wished very much to go to the dance, but none could go who had not beautiful clothes to wear.

The next three days everybody was busy in Salt village. The men brought out rich blankets and made their moccasins white with powdered clay. The women combed their hair or baked heaps of fresh meal cakes for the feast. All were gay and happy.

On the fourth day was the dance. As the little maiden drove her Turkeys to the field she saw the villagers getting ready to go. They were dressed in bright blankets and had eagles' feathers in their hair.

The little maiden looked down at her own ragged blanket. Tears came into her eyes.

"They will never let me go to the dance in this ragged blanket," she said.

TURKEY GOBBLER

But that morning a strange thing happened. When the little maiden came to the field her Turkeys did not seem to want to feed. They stood around, clucking and gobbling to one another as if they wanted to talk.

At last an old Gobbler came strutting up to the little maiden. His big tail was spread and his wings hung down and hid his legs like a skirt.

"Maiden mother," he said, "we know you want to go to the dance. Now we will help you."

The little maiden was astonished, — she had never heard Turkeys talk before; but the old Gobbler went on: "Listen! At noon we Turkeys will begin to cluck and gobble. You must then drive us back to the village. When we come into our cage we will show you what to do."

The little maiden could not understand how Turkeys could talk, but she promised to do as the old Gobbler said.

At noon, sure enough, the Turkeys began to cluck and gobble, and the little maiden drove them to the village. When they came to the

WOODEN CAGE, OR PEN

wooden cage the old Gobbler made the other Turkeys go inside. Last of all, he went in and called to the little maiden, "Come into our house!"

The little maiden went into the cage and sat down. All the Turkeys stood around her in a circle.

"Give me your blanket," said the old Gobbler.

The little maiden took off her old ragged blanket and laid it on the floor.

The old Gobbler pulled it with his beak until it was flat like a mat. He spread his big tail and dropped his wings again like a skirt. Then he began to dance back and forth over the blanket.

In a little while he stopped dancing and picked the blanket up in his beak. He swelled out his breast, put back his head, and puffed. When he laid the blanket down again it was a beautiful white mantle.

Another old Turkey now stepped out of the circle, and the little maiden gave him another piece of her clothing. When he had danced and puffed, it, also, was clean and beautiful. And so, piece by piece, all the little maiden's clothing was made clean and bright.

Then all the Turkeys spread their tails and began to dance around the little maiden.

"Do not move! You must sit while we dance," they cried.

They clucked and gobbled and flirted their tails as they danced. Whenever they passed close to the little maiden they brushed her with their wings.

When the dance was ended the little maiden's face was round and beautiful; her cheeks were plump; her hair was now soft and wavy.

But the old Gobbler had not finished. He stepped out of the circle again and stood before the little maiden.

"Maiden mother, you have no necklace. Perhaps I can find you one," he said.

He spread his tail and wings and began to dance. Then he put back his head and coughed. In a moment a fine shell necklace came up into his mouth.

ZUÑI GIRL WITH NECKLACE AND EARRINGS

Another Turkey danced and coughed and two blue earrings came into his mouth; he dropped them at the little maiden's feet.

Then the old Gobbler spoke once more.

"Maiden mother, now you are beautiful and have rich clothing; but sometimes people become proud and forget those who helped them. Do not forget us. Come back to us before the sun sets. Leave the cage door open as you go."

The little maiden placed the necklace about her neck and put the earrings in her ears. She thanked the Turkeys many times.

As she went out she left the cage door open. The Turkeys called after her through the door: "Maiden mother, remember! Do not forget us."

"Dear Turkeys, I will remember," she answered.

Then, as she hurried away, they called again: "Maiden mother, remember! Come back to us before the sun sets."

"Dear Turkeys, I will remember," she answered.

When the little maiden came to the place of the dance no one thought she was the poor Turkey maiden. Her mantle was the richest and whitest at the dance.

All the young men smiled when they looked at her. They thought her the most beautiful maiden they had ever seen.

"Who can she be?" they asked.

The old men invited her to come into the dance, and all joined hands in a great circle. All the young men wanted to be next to her and hold the little maiden's hand. She was very happy.

When the dance was ended the old men called for another. Thus the afternoon went by. The little maiden had never had such a happy time. She forgot all about her Turkeys.

At last the dancing was nearly over. As they joined hands for the last time the little maiden looked up. The sun was just setting in the West.

Then the little maiden thought of her Turkeys.

"O my dear Turkeys, I have forgotten you!" she cried.

She sprang out of the dance and ran back toward the village. The old men called to her, but she would not stop.

In the West the sun had set behind the mountains. It was growing dark.

Swiftly the little maiden ran to the wooden cage. It was empty.

Down the path she turned to the big field. Far off she could hear the Turkeys running over the hard ground. She listened. The Turkeys were singing:

> "Maiden mother,
> Maiden mother,
>   You forgot us!
> Maiden mother,
> Maiden mother,
>   Now we leave you!"

"Dear Turkeys, come back to me!" cried the little maiden.

She ran and ran; but the Turkeys spread their wings and flew away toward the mountains.

The little maiden looked down at her white mantle. It was soiled and ragged, and its border was torn. As she ran she had cut her moccasins on the sharp stones. Now they were full of holes.

Her shell necklace had broken and fallen from her neck. She

had lost her earrings.

The little maiden hid her face in her hands. Hot tears rolled down her cheeks. Sobbing, she turned to go back to the village.

As she went she could hear the Turkeys singing far away:

"Maiden mother,

Maiden mother,

You forgot us!

Maiden mother,

Maiden mother,

Now we leave you!"

XVII

THE FLYING HEAD

This is the tale of the Flying Head

Which makes the red man shudder with dread

When the storm wind screams on a wintry night

And he tells this tale by the lodge-fire light.

The Flying Head was a fearful thing

That flew on the blasts which the tempests bring

When the roaring hurricane tears the trees

And lashes the ocean and beats the seas.

The Flying Head had flaming eyes,

Round and staring, of hideous size;

And great white teeth that bit the air,

And round red mouth as big as a bear.

His feet were two great hairy paws;

And hair hung down from his bony jaws;

And when in the tempest he rode the air,

His wings were his long black locks of hair.

One night, in her wigwam, on her mat,

A lonely Indian widow sat,

And heard the storm roar high and higher,

While she baked chestnuts by the fire.

As over the coals for the nuts she bent,

The Flying Head peeped into her tent

And thought that the fire coals, glowing hot,

Were the new-baked chestnuts that she sought.

"Hu, hu!" he growled, "I am hungry, too;

I have tasted nothing the whole night through;

But these red things in a heap that lie, —

If the woman can eat them, why not I?"

Then into the wigwam he came with a leap,

And opened his mouth to the red fire heap,

And, ere the woman could start or call,

He had swallowed the fire heap, coals and all.

But the red coals hot in his body lay

And boiled and sizzled and burned away,

Till the Flying Head with a roar of pain

Leaped out into the night again.

But what became of the Flying Head

When out of the widow's tent door he fled

Was never known to the Indian men,

For none of them ever saw him again.

XVIII

OLD WINTER MAN AND THE SPRING MAIDEN

On the edge of a forest stood a birch-bark wigwam. Its roof curved over like the back of a bow.

In a fireplace on the floor some coals were burning. A little smoke went up through the smoke hole in the roof.

An old man sat by the fire. He had a mat under him and a wolf-skin robe over his shoulders. On the floor near by lay a small heap of dry sticks.

He was a queer looking old man. His hair was white like frost. His face was wrinkled and he had a round hump on his back.

The old man took a stick from the heap and put it on the fire. Soon there was a blaze. The light made the old man's face look yellow. The black smoke made shadows on the roof overhead.

In the forest outside the winter wind was blowing.

Hu—u–u–u! it roared through the trees.

The old man put another stick on the fire. Evening was near and it was growing dark. The wind still blew outside. The wigwam shook and rattled in the storm.

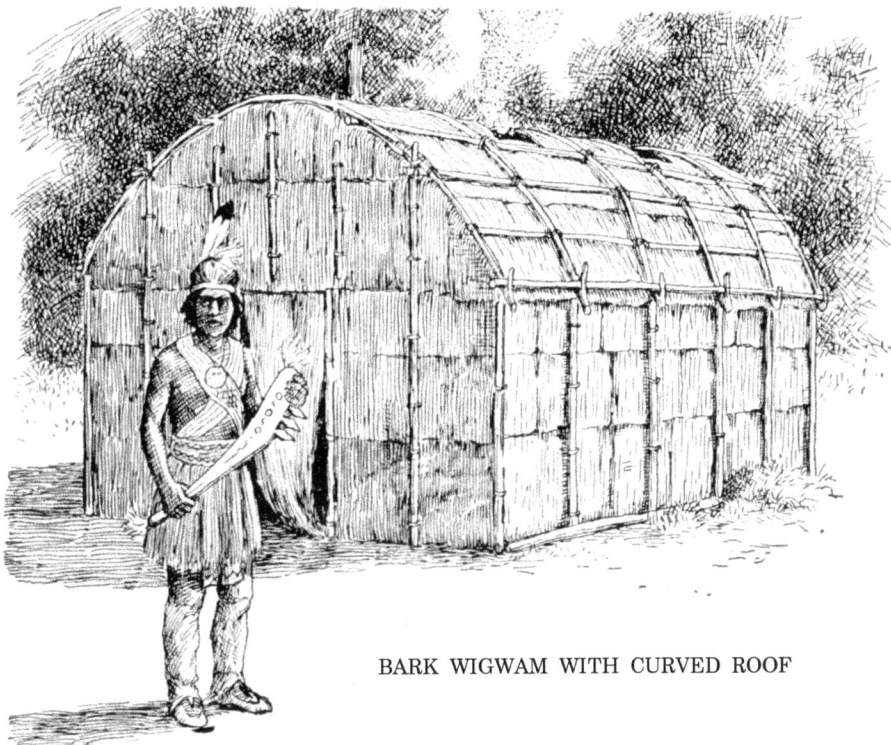

BARK WIGWAM WITH CURVED ROOF

All night the old man sat by the fire. He drew his mat close to the fireplace, for he was cold. The wind came down the smoke hole and blew ashes into his face. Before morning he had put his last stick on the fire.

"It is my last stick; when it is burned the fire will die," he said.

He rested his head on his arm and shut his eyes. He was very tired. His white hair fell down and hid his face. In the ashes the fire was dying.

Outside in the forest the wind still blew.

Hu—u–u–u–u! it roared through the trees.

Suddenly the old man raised his head.

"I thought I heard footsteps," he said.

He put his hand to his ear and listened. Again he heard the footsteps faintly in the storm. *Tread, tread,* they went around the wigwam.

A bearskin curtain hung over the door. As the old man listened some one pushed the curtain aside. The old man looked up. A maiden stood in the doorway.

She was a beautiful maiden. Her cheeks were painted red and her long black hair fell almost to her feet.

Flowers covered her head. Her robe was made of sweet grasses and her moccasins of lily leaves sewed together.

The maiden stood in the doorway and smiled. The morning sun peeped over the hills and a little sunlight came in through the door. The wind did not blow so hard now.

The old man frowned, for he did not like the sunlight; but he spoke to the maiden and asked her to come in.

"Come and tell me who you are," he said. "I am old Winter Man. I bring the snow and cold."

The maiden smiled and came into the wigwam.

"I am the Spring Maiden. I bring the warm winds and the sweet flowers," she said.

The old man looked at her and frowned. He did not like the warm winds and the flowers.

"You must go away," he said. "If you do not, I shall frighten you with my cold."

He filled the earthen bowl of his pipe and lighted it with a coal. He blew little clouds of smoke from his nostrils.

EARTHEN PIPE

Then he spoke: "When I blow my breath the white frost falls. The lakes and rivers are covered with ice."

The maiden smiled.

"When I breathe, the air grows warm," she said. "The ice melts on the lakes and rivers."

The warm sunlight poured through the door and fell on the old man's face. He frowned and spoke again: "When I shake my white hair the air is filled with snow. Soon the earth is covered with snow. Everything is covered with snow."

The maiden smiled and answered: "When I shake my hair the warm rain falls. Soon the snow is melted and the earth is green again."

The old man's hand trembled as he put the pipe from his lips.

The robe had slipped from his shoulders and he looked at the maiden with frightened eyes; but he spoke once more: "When I walk in the forest, cold winds blow. Leaves fall from the trees, and the grasses die, for winter comes."

The maiden smiled again and answered: "When I walk in the forest the warm sun shines. The trees put out leaves, and flowers spring up, for spring is here."

As she spoke she stepped to the old man's side and touched him. Then a wonderful thing happened.

The old man's head nodded. His eyes closed, and he fell upon the floor. He began to grow smaller.

Water ran out of his mouth; his white hair melted and ran away. His robe turned into a heap of vines. The wigwam roof fell in.

The maiden went out into the fields and forests. Warm winds blew. The trees put out leaves. Wherever the maiden stepped flowers sprung up.

And each year at springtime the trees put out leaves. Flowers still spring up in the fields where the maiden stepped.

CHILDREN'S SUPPLEMENT

A YOUNG AMERICAN

THINGS FOR CHILDREN TO MAKE

STONE AX

Axes and hammers were made of stone and were pecked into shape with a hard quartz pebble. Fig. 1 is an ax; Fig. 2 is a hammer. They may be shaped from modeling clay or from blocks of soft pine.

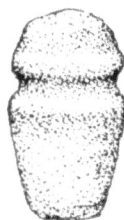 

FIG. 1   FIG. 2

To haft them, take a tough green stick (Fig. 3); shave the end *A* thin and flat; draw the flat portion around the groove of the ax (Fig. 4); bind neatly, as in Fig. 5.

FIG. 3

The Indians often sewed a piece of wet rawhide over the handle. When the rawhide dried it contracted and made the handle firm. This, however, is not essential.

FIG. 4   FIG. 5

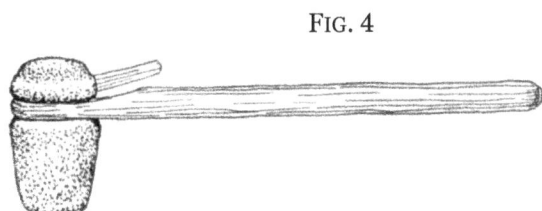 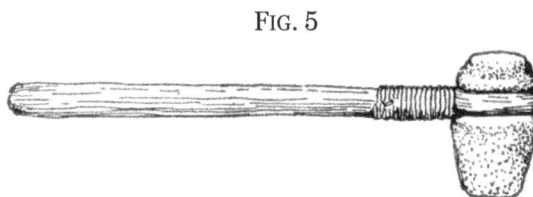

THE DAKOTA TENT, OR TEPEE [1]

Wigwam is an Algonkin word meaning "lodge," or "dwelling." Among the Algonkin tribes this was usually a cabin-like structure of poles and bark, or a dome-shaped tent of the same material. The name is now commonly applied to any of the tent or cabin-like lodges of our Indians.

Many kinds of lodges were in use in the different tribes. The Dakota movable tent, or tepee, is the best known form. A small model is easily made.

[1] Tē´ pēē.

Take a dozen willow sticks, or other wood, twelve inches in length and the thickness of a small lead pencil. With a longer willow make a hoop ten inches in diameter (Fig. 6).

Lay the hoop upon a table. Tie ten of the willow sticks to the hoop at regular intervals. These will form the tent poles.

FIG. 6

Draw the tops together and tie them two inches from the ends at *A* (Fig. 7). This will make the frame of the tent.

For the tent cover cut a semicircular piece from a strip of white muslin, as in Fig. 8. The diameters *AB, AD,* and *AC* should measure ten inches each.

Cut out two triangular pieces, *AFE* and *ARG. AE* and *AG* are each an inch long. *EF, AF, AR,* and *GR* measure each two inches.

With a pair of scissors make the cuts *PY* and *QZ*. Each should be a half inch in length.

The pieces *HLMJ* and *IONK* are for smoke flaps. *HJ* should measure five inches; *LM,* four inches; *HL,* two inches; and *MJ,* one inch. The same measurements apply to *IONK.*

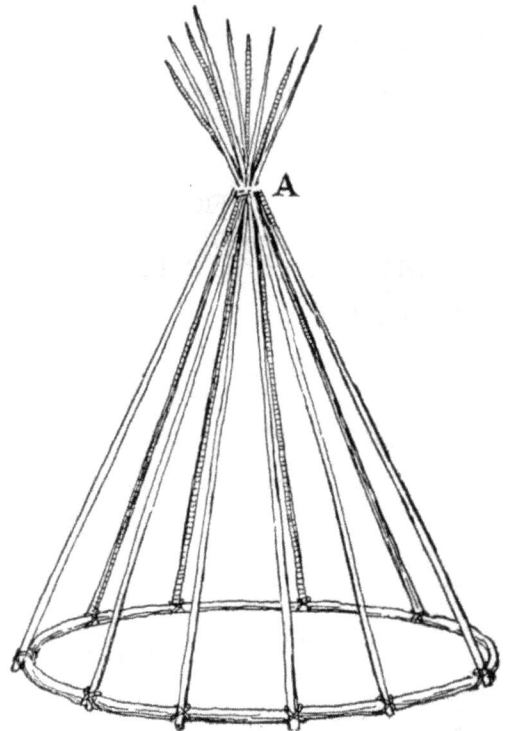

FIG. 7

In the corners of the smoke flaps, *H* and *I,* sew two small, three-cornered pieces for pockets.

Sew the smoke flaps to the tent cover so that *ML* is fitted to *PE,* and *NO* to *QG.*

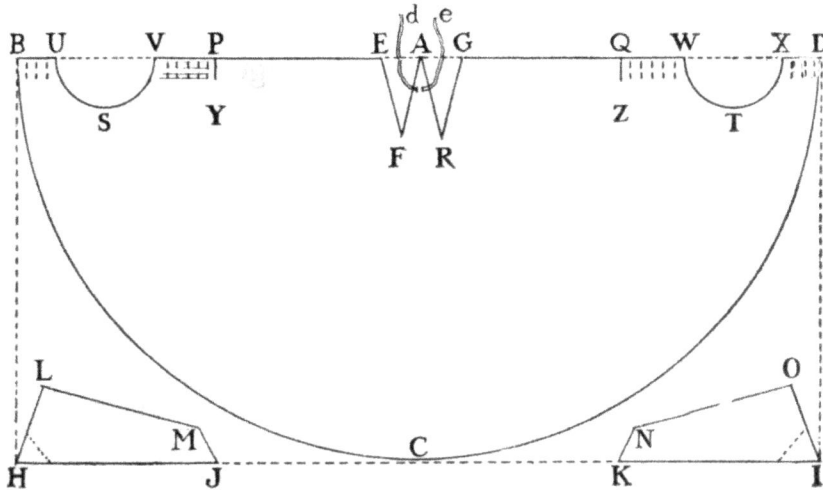

FIG. 8

Cut out two half-circular pieces *S* and *T.* The diameters *UV* and *WX* should measure two and a half inches each. *BU* and *DX* should be one inch each.

Above and below the door, between *P* and *B,* and *Q* and *D,* make a double row of holes near the edge of the cover. These are the lacing holes.

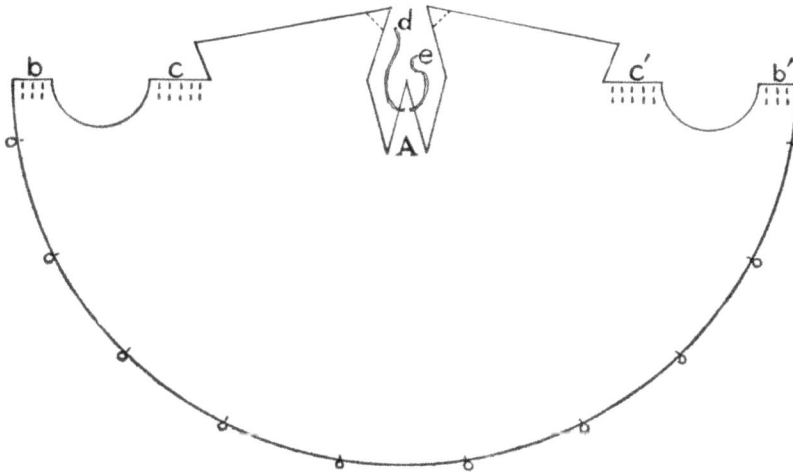

FIG. 9

Around the circular edge sew ten small loops of cord or small twine. In the triangular piece *AFR* sew a small cord *de.* The tent cover will now appear as in Fig. 9.

To put the cover on the frame, tie the three-cornered piece *A* (Fig. 9), with the cord *de,* to one of the willow poles at *A* (Fig. 7).

FIG. 10

Draw the edges *b* and *b'* and *c* and *c'* (Fig. 9) together, and lace with wooden pins. Cut these from twigs or match stems, one inch in length, as in Fig. 10.

Tie the cover to the hoop through the loops sewed to the lower edge.

Two of the willow sticks remain unused. Thrust the fore ends into the pockets of the smoke flaps and fasten behind to the hoop. These keep the smoke flaps in place. The tent now appears as in Fig. 11.

For door flap, bend a small willow rod or a wire in the shape of a horse-shoe (Fig. 12).

FIG. 11

Cover with a bit of muslin sewed or glued over the rod. Hang by a string to the lacing pin just over the door, as in Fig. 13.

FIG. 12

A tent for camp use may be made by increasing the measurements to feet instead of inches.

The base hoop will not then be needed, as the tent poles are thrust into the ground. The loops on the tent cover are made fast to the ground with wooden pins.

The tent poles of many Dakota lodges measure thirty feet in length.

In old times there was a prescribed way in which a tepee

FIG. 13

106

should be set up. It was symbolic of the powers that surround man, — a kind of little acted prayer that the new-made home be kept from harm.

INDIAN DRESS

The Indian dress was of buckskin. It consisted of leggings, shirt, belt, and clout. The last two may be omitted.

The dress is easily imitated in yellow cambric. Cut shirt and leggings to fit the child.

By folding the cloth, the leggings (Fig. 14) may be made with a single seam, *AB*. The outer edges are fringed. Let the cloth project two inches beyond the seam. Cut the fringe with a pair of scissors, as shown in the illustration.

The shirt, or coat (Fig. 15), is a simple garment. It opens from the neck over the shoulders. It is fringed at the sides and under the arms.

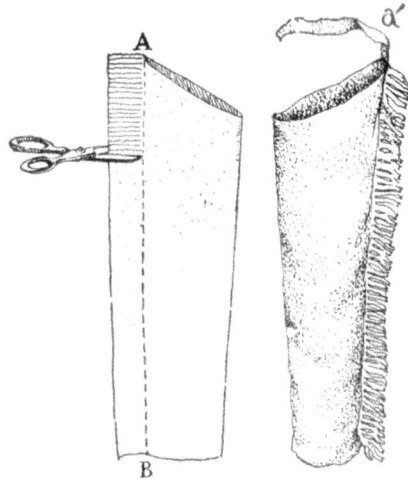

FIG. 14

Draw the leggings and shirt over the boy's other clothing. Fasten to the latter with safety pins.

The Indian way was to lace the shirt at the shoulders and fasten the legging to the belt with a thong, *a'* (Fig. 14).

A bright-colored blanket will do for a girl's costume. It should be thrown over the shoulders and fastened about the waist with a belt.

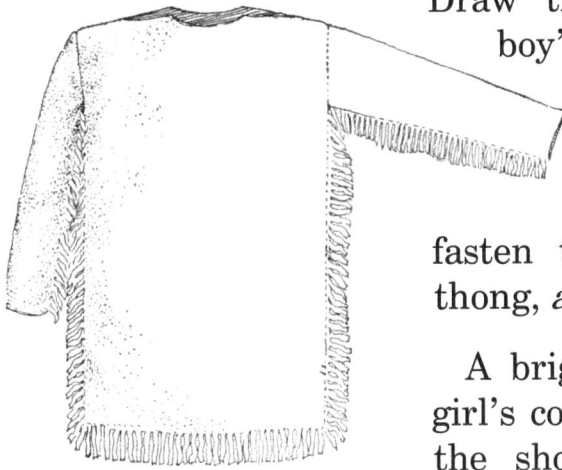

FIG. 15

When full costume is used the face may be painted. Rub the skin well with vaseline and use Venetian red. The whole face is painted for boys, but only the cheeks for girls.

Indians did not paint the face or body for mere ornament, or for fun. Each color had a meaning and had to do with religious thoughts.

CLAY POT

FIG. 16

The Indian cooking pot was shaped like Fig. 16. It was made of well-worked clay, mixed with a little sand to avoid cracking in drying. The children can mold a pot in modeling clay or in ordinary yellow clay. The Indians rolled a lump of the wet clay in the palms until they had a slender rod or pencil. They worked this into the growing pot by coiling it around the edge (Fig. 17).

If common clay is used the pot may be dried and then burned for an hour in a wood fire.

FIG. 17

BOW AND ARROW

Fig. 18 represents an Indian bow. It may be made of ash or hickory, and should be a little more than half the height of the child.

The arrow is half the length of the bow, or shorter. For a child's arrow the Indians shaved down a sapling, leaving one end blunt, as

FIG. 18

108

in Fig. 19. This was less dangerous than arrows pointed with flint.

An arrow is useless unless feathered. Trim two turkey feathers, as in Fig. 20, two inches in length. Bind neatly to the shaft of the arrow, as in Figs. 19 and 20. This method is simpler than that of using three feathers glued to the shaft.

The nock *A* (Fig. 20) is to receive the string. A little silk bound around the shaft of the arrow just below the nock will prevent the arrow from splitting.

Bows and arrows should be used by children with great care.

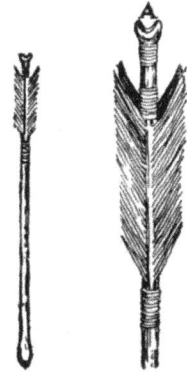

FIG. 19 FIG. 20

MOCCASINS

There are different forms of the moccasin, or Indian shoe. That of the prairie tribes has three parts, — sole, upper, and tongue. The sole is of thick rawhide; the tongue and upper are of buckskin.

For indoor wear, use white canvas for the tongue and upper. The sole may be cut from a piece of very thick felt.

It is best to begin by cutting out a pattern.

Let the child place his right foot, with the shoe removed, upon a piece of cardboard. Draw outline with a pencil and cut out with a pair of scissors, as in Fig. 21.

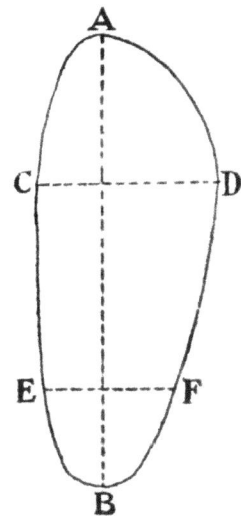

FIG. 21

From another piece of cardboard cut out Fig. 22 for the upper. The sole and upper cut by these patterns will be for the right foot. For the left, turn the patterns over.

For a child seven years of age the length of the sole, *AB* (Fig. 21), should be eight inches; width, *CD*, three and a half inches; width of heel, *EF*, two and a half inches.

109

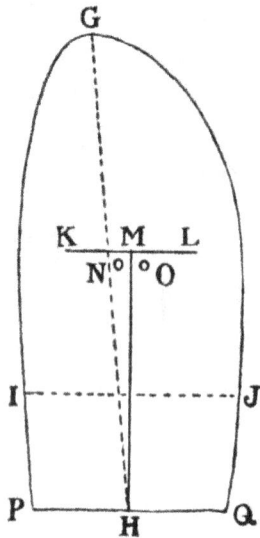

FIG. 22

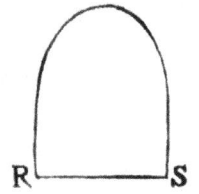

FIG. 23

The upper (Fig. 22) should measure nine inches at *GH*; width, *IJ*, four and a half inches.

Make the cuts *KL* and *MH* with a pair of scissors. The first should be halfway between the toe and heel and should be three inches in length.

In the corners *N* and *O* pierce two holes. In these put a small leather string for lacing.

Sew the upper on the sole, beginning at the toe. The heel is made by sewing *HP* and *HQ* together. If the moccasin is turned wrong side out before sewing, the seams will be neater.

Cut out the tongue (Fig. 23) from a piece of canvas, three and a half inches long and three inches at the base *RS*. Sew to the upper so that *RS* shall join *KL*.

The completed moccasin is shown in Fig. 24.

The Indians embroider their moccasins with beautiful beadwork or with stained quills of the porcupine. A pretty effect, not unlike embroidery, may be given by using thick velvet instead of canvas for the uppers. Blue, red, and yellow are the favorite colors.

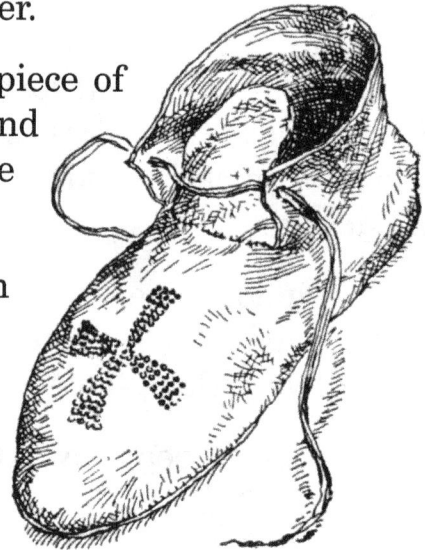

FIG. 24

When canvas is used, beadwork may be imitated by cutting out designs in bright-colored cloth and sewing or even gluing to the uppers.

Fig. 25 is a common Dakota design. It represents the four cardinal points.

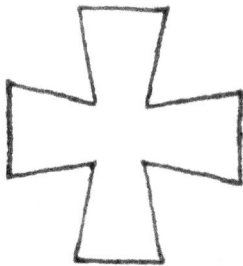

FIG. 25

Before white man came, the Indians had no domestic beasts except dogs. These were trained to drag a kind of vehicle called a "travois." On this were packed the household goods whenever camp was moved.

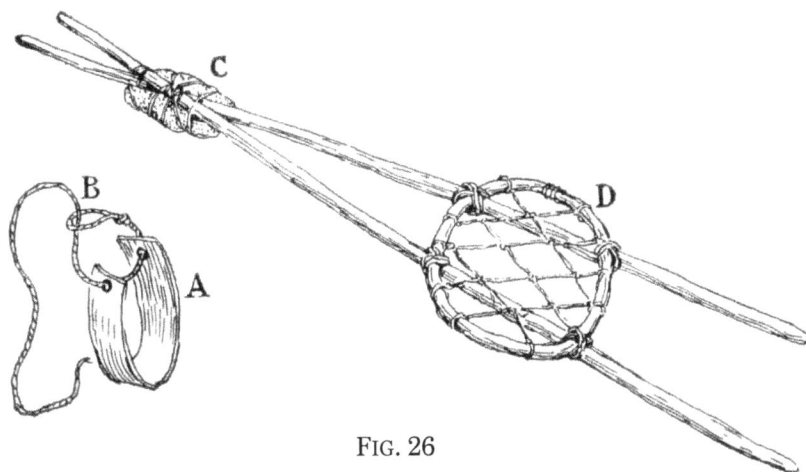

FIG. 26

The travois is made with collar and thong, two light poles, a basket, and a pad. The collar and thong are of rawhide (*A, B,* Fig. 26). The two poles are lashed at the smaller end, and the joint is covered with a pad of soft leather, *C,* stuffed with hair. The basket *D* is a willow hoop with a simple netting.

FIG. 27

To harness the travois, the lashed ends of the poles are slipped into the noose of the thong *B* (Fig. 26), and the noose drawn taut.

The thong is whipped twice or thrice around one of the poles and tied. It is then passed under the dog's body and tied again to the opposite pole, thus forming a girth. The harnessed dog is shown in Fig. 27.

If better materials are wanting the collar may be made of felt or of thick canvas. A twine or a leather shoestring will do for a thong, and willow sticks for poles. The latter should be two and a half times the length of the dog's body, measuring from the nose to the root of the tail.

Children will be interested to know that the travois basket often held a dark-eyed Indian baby.

WAR BONNET

The war bonnet, or ceremonial headdress, was made with eagles' feathers. These were fastened in a circle to a cap of buffalo skin.

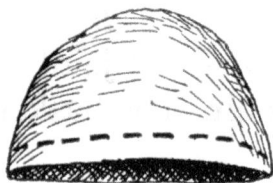

FIG. 28

A good imitation of a native war bonnet can easily be made.

Take an old hat of soft felt, cut off the brim, and remove the band (Fig. 28).

Get a dozen or more tail feathers of a turkey, — those of a white turkey are the prettiest.

Cut the shaft of each feather to a point, as in Fig. 29. With a small knife pierce two openings in the crown, just

A

FIG. 29

FIG. 30

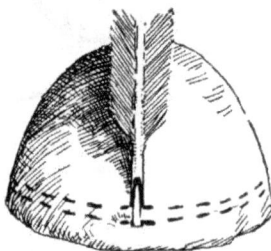

FIG. 31

FIG. 32

above the rim. Thrust the point of the quill *A* (Fig. 29) through the openings, as in Fig. 30, and double the point back into the hollow shaft, as in Fig. 31. This secures the feather to the felt crown.

Sew or tie a bit of red flannel around the base of the quill, as in Fig. 32.

Continue this process until the felt crown is surrounded with a circlet of feathers (Fig. 33). Fix these in place with a thread *B,* drawn through the shafts of the feathers with a needle.

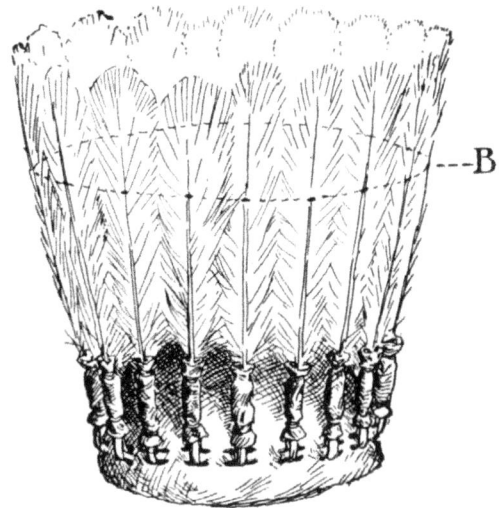

FIG. 33

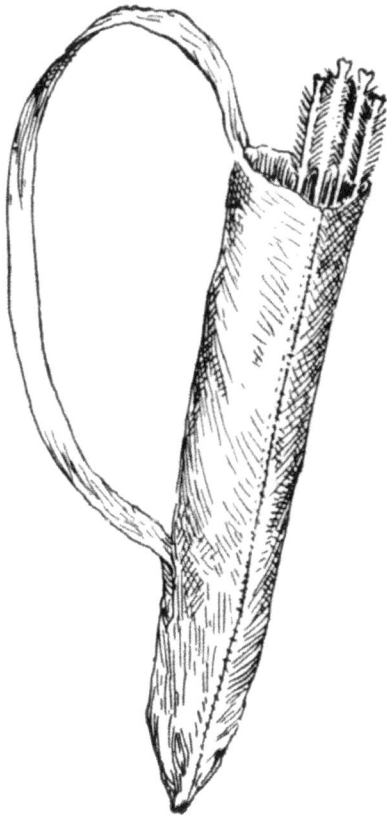

FIG. 34

QUIVER

The simplest form of quiver is shown in Fig. 34. Cut from canvas to fit size of arrows. It should rest on the right shoulder, held in place by a thong or belt. The latter should pass over the right shoulder and under the left arm.

THE PIPE

The Indians carved beautiful pipes from soapstone or red pipestone.

Fig. 35 shows the common form.

FIG. 35

FIG. 36

The stem (Fig. 36) is a piece of ash sapling from which the pith has been removed.

A pipe may be molded in modeling clay. A pine stick, cut like Fig. 36, will do for a stem.

The bowl may be made six inches in length, and the stem ten inches.

When smoking, the Indians sat on the ground, as in Fig. 37. In council they usually sat in a circle, and the pipe was passed from mouth to mouth.

FIG. 37

EXPLANATORY NOTES

I. LITTLE UGLY BOY

Tribe, Zuñi; **home,** western New Mexico

Zuñi houses are built of stone and are entered through a trapdoor in the roof. A ladder reaches from the roof to the ground. In times of danger the ladder is drawn up, making the house into a kind of fort.

As the houses are built in a solid block, the flat roofs serve for a court. It was quite natural for little Ugly Boy to address the villagers from his grandmother's roof.

II. WHY TURKEYS HAVE RED EYES

Tribe, Oto; **home,** southeastern Nebraska

This is, to an Indian, a highly moral tale. The unbecoming curiosity of the Turkeys and of the old Rabbit grandmother is properly punished.

Indians recorded important events by a rude kind of picture writing. Songs were often written in these picture symbols. Such, perhaps, are what the little Rabbit claimed to have in his robe.

Indian picture writing is described in Section XIV of Longfellow's *Hiawatha.*

III. THE SUN MAN AND THE MOON

Tribe, Omaha; **home,** eastern and central Nebraska

This is a quaint bit of Indian humor. Explain how the face, or part of the Moon that is light, is always turned toward the Sun. Perhaps it is because the Moon *is watching* the Sun as she follows him through the sky.

115

The Omahas and some other tribes built houses of split logs covered with clay. Such lodges were roomy and a good shelter against cold. Our western sod houses are thought by some to be modeled after these earth lodges.

IV. WUCHOWSON THE WIND BLOWER

Tribe, Passamaquoddy; **home,** about Passamaquoddy Bay, Maine

The pemmican which the Indian took as he started North was for food on the way. It was made of dried meat pounded fine and mixed with boiling fat. This was poured while hot into skin bags. A handful of pemmican lasted a traveler for a day.

V. THE LITTLE ICE MAN

Tribe, Cherokee; **home,** mountainous region of Tennessee, Georgia, and Alabama

It will be noted that the chief addresses the old man in the council house as *grandfather.* This is a term of respect, — a common use of Indian kinship names. Generally our Indians had much respect for the aged.

Indians provided themselves with new moccasins before starting on a journey. Sometimes they even took extra pairs along.

The place of honor in a wigwam is that farthest from the door, on the opposite side of the fire. A seat here in winter time is warmest, and gives a ready view of any one entering the door.

VI. GLOOSKAP AND THE WINTER GIANT

Tribe, Micmac; **home,** New Brunswick, Nova Scotia, and islands of the Gulf of St. Lawrence

When a deer was brought home it was left on the ground outside the wigwam. The women then went out and dressed the carcass.

It was proper for the Indian host to hand a lighted pipe to his guests. When they had smoked with him, he was bound by the same ties that bind an Arab to one who has eaten his salt. For the Winter Giant to harm one who had smoked his pipe was a violation of sacred hospitality.

The time for story-telling was the long winter evenings. It was therefore fitting that the Winter Giant should entertain Glooskap with wonderful tales.

VII. THE FISHER WHO LET OUT SUMMER

Tribe, Chippewa; **home,** regions about Lake Superior

The Fisher is a fur-bearing animal of the weasel family. It is about the size of a cat.

It is said that the Chippewas have never made pottery. They carved bowls from wood or made them of birch bark. The household utensils of a wigwam are not numerous. For this reason it is still the custom among the Chippewas for each guest to bring his own eating bowl when invited to a feast.

For the Otter to laugh at the awkwardness of his host was in the highest degree discourteous. Hence the ill luck that pursued him.

The Fisher lying among the stars is the constellation of Charles's Wain, or the Big Dipper.

VIII. THE RAINBOW SNAKE

Tribe, Shoshoni; **home,** western Wyoming and neighboring regions

"No longer the rose pods grow." The Shoshonis did not plant corn. The seed pods of the wild rose were boiled and eaten by many of our western tribes.

IX. LITTLE SCAR FACE

Tribe, Micmac; **home,** New Brunswick, Nova Scotia, and islands of
the Gulf of St. Lawrence

Every Indian village had its council house, which served much
the same purpose as a New England townhall.

The sledge is the familiar *toboggan.* It was made of strips of
wood lashed together with thongs.

Mr. Leland believes this to be an old solar myth worked up with
a part of the story of Cinderella. The latter could have been
learned from the Canadian French.

Team means "moose," and by the Micmacs is pronounced in two
syllables. The author has ventured to anglicize it to one.

X. HOW THE LITTLE RABBIT SNARED THE SUN

Tribe, Omaha; **home,** eastern and central Nebraska

The snare is a simple noose set in places where animals are wont
to run. The Omahas lived in a prairie country where forest
growths are found only along water courses. In such woodlands
animals often made paths in going to water.

XI. THE MAGIC WIGWAM

Tribe, Passamaquoddy; **home,** about Passamaquoddy Bay, Maine

It is not long since every New England farmer laid in winter
provisions of smoked meat, dried berries and sweet corn, and maple
sugar.

The partridge is the ruffed grouse which feeds on the tender
buds of the birch. The New England Indians used birch bark as a
covering for their wigwams. This has a whitish appearance like
snow.

XII. WHY THE BABY SAYS "GOO"

Tribe, Penobscot; **home,** valley of the Penobscot, Maine

Maple sugar was an important article of diet with the New England Indians, who taught the art of making it to the whites. The sap was collected in wooden troughs and was boiled into sirup by dropping into it red-hot stones.

XIII. THE WREN

Tribe, Cherokee; **home,** mountainous region of Tennessee, Georgia and Alabama

Hominy was made of maize, or Indian corn. The kernels were broken in a wooden mortar. Making hominy was girls' and women's work.

A small bow was put into the hands of every Indian boy. With this he was taught to shoot birds and small game. Hence the birds' lament.

XIV. THE GOOD GIANTS

Tribe, Micmac; **home,** New Brunswick, Nova Scotia, and islands of the Gulf of St. Lawrence

The little dog pointing out land over the ocean is not wholly a myth. "Lieutenant Colonel Kennan . . . had an Eskimo dog which in the thickest fog would scent the land at a great distance and continually point to it" (Leland).

Dogs were domesticated by all the Indian tribes. They were used as beasts of burden and as watch-dogs. Their flesh was eaten by many tribes.

119

XV. THE LITTLE FAWN

Tribe, Omaha; **home,** eastern and central Nebraska

A deer's color is protective and blends with that of the thickets which the animal haunts. The under part of the tail, however, is white. When deer are frightened the tail is raised and the white "flag" is shown. In this way the members of the herd are able to follow one another.

A little fawn running with "flag" exposed makes a very funny sight.

Deer when startled give a kind of shrill snort. This is called the "whistle."

XVI. THE TURKEY MAIDEN

Tribe, Zuñi; **home,** western New Mexico

Turkeys were domesticated by the Mexican tribes. They were brought to Europe by the Spanish.

In old times the Zuñis owned large flocks of them. They were plucked for their feathers, like geese. The feathers were used in making the famous feather cloth.

Mantles of native cotton, such as the little Turkey Maiden wore, are still woven by the Zuñis. They are often beautifully embroidered.

XVII. THE FLYING HEAD

Tribe, Iroquois; **home,** central and northern New York

The Flying Head is the personification of the whirlwind or cyclone.

XVIII. OLD WINTER MAN AND THE SPRING MAIDEN

Tribe, Iroquois; **home,** central and northern New York

The Iroquois wigwam was a cabin of birch or elm bark. The door usually faced the rising sun and was closed by the skin of a deer or a bear. Stout-woven mats of rushes were spread upon the floor.

Such wigwams were apt to be smoky, but otherwise were fairly comfortable and warm.

For the Chippewa or Ojibway form of this myth, see Section II of *Hiawatha.*

BOOK TWO

INDIAN HERO TALES

INDIAN HERO TALES

RETOLD BY

GILBERT L. WILSON, Ph.D.

FIELD COLLECTOR FOR
AMERICAN MUSEUM OF NATURAL HISTORY
CITY OF NEW YORK

Illustrated by

FREDERICK N. WILSON

REG. U. S. PAT. OFF.

AMERICAN BOOK COMPANY
NEW YORK   CINCINNATI   CHICAGO

Original title page from the 1916 edition

FOREWORD

by Gilbert L. Wilson

THE Indian tribes of New England and Nova Scotia were called Abnaki, or East-land folk, by their Algonkin relatives; and Tarrateens, by our Puritan fathers. They played no small part in early New England history. Massasoit, Samoset, Uncas, Canonchet, King Philip, were Abnakis.

Small remnants of these tribes remain on New England soil. The Penobscots of Old Town, Maine, and the Passamaquoddies about Passamaquoddy Bay still hold to their language and many ancient customs. They number a few hundreds. The Micmacs, four thousand souls, chiefly in Nova Scotia, are as numerous as they were four centuries ago.

Indians believe in many gods and spirits; but no one of these is a Great Spirit, in the sense in which we use the term. However, every tribe has some legend of a creator, or first-maker, to whom the tribe owes its origin.

Glooskap is the Abnaki creator. His name means Deceiver; for when he forsook earth, Glooskap promised to return, but has not done so.

Two considerable collections of Abnaki myths have been made. The Rev. Silas Rand, fifty years a missionary to the Micmacs, recorded legends of that tribe; they were published after his death in 1894. In 1883 and 1884, Charles G. Leland collected legends from the Penobscot and Passamaquoddy tribes, publishing them in 1885. These two collections are authorities for most of the tales in this book. For the eighth tale, MacLean's "Canadian Savage Folk," and for the tenth tale, the "Tenth Annual Report of the Bureau of Ethnology," are authorities.

The illustrations in this book are from drawings by the author's brother. Many are from sketches made in the summer of 1912 when the author and his brother were making studies among the Hidatsa Indians for the American Museum of Natural History. Artist and author acknowledge courtesy of Professors M. R. Harrington, Frank G. Speck, W. H. Mechling, and W. C. Orchard of the University of Pennsylvania, in furnishing information or photographs; of Dr. Edward Sapir and Mr. Harlan Smith of the Canadian Geological Survey, who loaned photographic studies of Abnaki arts; and of Dr. Clark Wissler of the American Museum of Natural History.

FIRST TALE

THE COMING OF GLOOSKAP[1]

Long ago, a canoe came over the ocean. It was a wonderful canoe, made of stone, yet it rode the waves as lightly as a bird.

A warrior steered the canoe. He was tall, with great shoulders and thighs. An eagle's feather stood in his scalp lock.[2] It nodded as the warrior bent to his paddle.

The waves, beating on the hollow boat, made a sound like a drum. The warrior was singing:

[1] Gloōs - kăp   [2] See Note 1 at end of volume.

131

"I am Glooskap;

I come out of the east,

I come from the sunrise!"

The warrior steered to the shore, laid down his paddle, and leaped out on the beach.

He turned to the canoe. "Go!" he said. "When I have need, I will call you." And with his foot he gently pushed the bow.

The great canoe lurched, righted itself in the water, slowly turned, stopped. A wonderful thing then happened.

The canoe became an island of rock. Where the paddle had rested, rose a tall pine tree.

Thus Glooskap came to the land of the Abnakis.[1]

[1] Ăb - ná - kĭş

GLOOSKAP'S CANOE

SECOND TALE

THE MAKING OF MAN

It was a beautiful land. On the east lay the ocean. In the west were mountains. Rivers ran through green valleys; on their banks stood forests of birch, ash, and pine. The forests were full of game.

Glooskap looked upon the land. The sun had risen and was shining white over the ocean. Tall trees waved in the forests. Glooskap was pleased.

"It is a good land," he thought. "I will make man, and he shall dwell here; but no living thing must harm him!" He called the birds and beasts to a council in the forest.

They came, and he spoke to them. "I am going to make man;

133

but I must know that you cannot harm him, and I must name you!" He made them pass, one at a time, before him.

The bear came first, swaying his big haunches as he walked. "Your name is Mooin,"[1] Glooskap told him. "What would you do if you saw a man?"

"I should run!" said the bear.

"You shall live in the thickets," said Glooskap. "In winter, you may sleep in a hollow tree."

The moose came next. "Your name," said Glooskap, "shall be Teeam.[2] What would you do if you saw a man?"

The moose hung his head. "I should fear him," he said. "He will hunt me with snowshoes, in the deep snow!"

"And I should fear him," cried Quabeet,[3] the beaver, "for he will set traps to catch me!"

"You shall live," said Glooskap, "the one in the forests, the other in the streams."

[1] Mŏŏ - ĭn   [2] Tēé - ạm   [3] Quá - bēet

134

He called Meeko,[1] the squirrel. Meeko was the greatest of all the beasts.

"What would you do if you met a man?" Glooskap asked him.

"I would scratch down trees upon him!" barked Meeko.

Glooskap frowned, but lifted the squirrel in his arms and gently stroked his back. Meeko grew smaller and smaller, until he was as he is to-day.

"Now what would you do?" Glooskap asked.

"I would run up a tree," cried Meeko.

The land was at length ready for man.

Glooskap drew his bow, and sent an arrow singing among the trees. It struck an ash. The trunk split, and out sprang a warrior, young and handsome.

Again Glooskap shot, splitting an ash; and there stepped out a

[1] Meé - kō

135

young woman, with shining eyes. So he shot until his quiver was empty, and there were many men and women in the land.

Glooskap looked upon them and was glad.

"You shall be my people," he told them; "I will teach you many things. You shall build canoes. You shall make traps and bows, and plant corn. And you shall be called Abnakis, or Men of the East, because your land lies nearest the sunrise."

THE LAND OF THE ABNAKIS

THIRD TALE

GLOOSKAP'S FAMILY

So Glooskap dwelt with the Abnakis. He taught them to build villages and sail canoes; to hunt and fish and plant corn; to bury their fish in their fields that the corn might grow.[1] All that they knew, they learned of him.

Sometimes he lived in their villages and was their chief. Again, he dwelt apart by the sea; or he pitched his wigwam on an island where it was hard to come to him even in a canoe.

Glooskap had no wife. An old woman mended his moccasins and kept his pot boiling. He called her his grandmother.[2] Her name was the Bear Woman.

[1] See Note 2 at end of volume.   [2] See Note 3.

And she could be a bear if she wanted; for everything was strange in those days. All the Abnakis were named for beasts or birds, and could turn into these when they willed.

A small lad played about Glooskap's wigwam and helped the old grandmother. His name was Abistanooch,[1] or the marten. Glooskap called him his younger brother.[2] Abistanooch could be a babe, a lad, or a young man, as he had need.

The little marten ate always from a birch-bark dish. If danger came nigh him, he had but to drop the dish and Glooskap, finding it, would know what to do.

These two, the Bear Woman and Abistanooch, were Glooskap's family. He had no kin of his own.

It was not always so. Malsum,[3] the wolf, was Glooskap's twin brother. But Malsum was wicked; he had caused his own mother's death. Glooskap was good.

---

[1] Ă - bĭs - tắ - nōōch   [2] See Note 4.   [3] M ắl - sŭm

The brothers had charmed lives; and each could be slain by one thing only. Neither knew what it was that could kill the other.

One day when they were children, they played at making lodges. As they sat and rested, Malsum asked, "Elder brother, what can slay you?"

Glooskap did not answer at once. "Malsum is wicked!" he thought; and he said aloud, "Do not strike me with an owl's feather!"

"I," said Malsum, "fear only a fern root!"

Years passed, and the brothers had grown to be men, when Quabeet, the beaver, tempted Malsum.

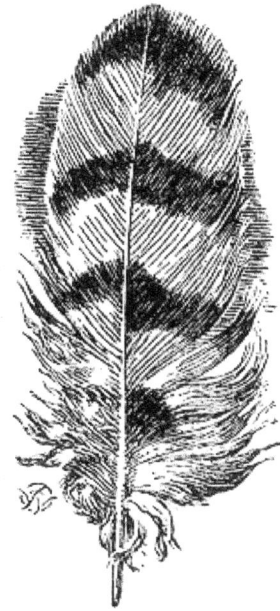

"All men love Glooskap," he whispered. "Slay him! Men will then obey you!"

Malsum listened to Quabeet. With his bow, he shot an owl and plucked out a feather; and when Glooskap slept, Malsum stole in and struck him.

The blow wakened Glooskap. He saw the feather and understood; but he hid his anger.

"Ho!" he laughed, "I dreamed I felt an owl's feather. Well for me it was not a pine root!"

Days went by, and Glooskap and his brother were on a hunt. By a brook where deer came to drink, they built them a hunting lodge and camped.

One morning while Glooskap was sleeping, Malsum dug up a pine root; he crept into the lodge and struck his brother.

Glooskap sprang up in anger. "Twice have you tried to slay me!" he cried. "No more shall you sleep in my wigwam!" And he

drove Malsum from the lodge.

But Glooskap was grieved; and he went out and sat by the brook. "Malsum hates me," he said aloud. "It is well he does not know that a cattail rush can slay me!"

In the reeds by the brook lay Quabeet, listening. When Glooskap had gone, Quabeet stole out and sought Malsum.

"I heard Glooskap talking," Quabeet told him. "He said a cattail rush can slay him!"

Malsum was overjoyed. "You bring me good news," he cried. "What now shall I give you!"

The beaver thought. "I am tired of the water," he said, "Give me wings that I may fly!"

But Malsum laughed aloud. "Begone!" he cried. And he drove the beaver into the brook.

Evening came, and Glooskap was boiling a kettle on a fire before his camp, when Quabeet crept out of the reeds and called to him: "Malsum knows your secret! He seeks to slay you with a cattail rush!"

Glooskap was sad at these words. He sat all night with his robe about his knees, thinking of his brother's wickedness. In the morning he dug a fern root, found Malsum, and slew him.

Then Glooskap mourned for Malsum. He put clay on his head, fasted, and sang a sad song; and he made a fire by his brother's grave,[1] and sat there.

[1] See Note 5.

GLOOSKAP MOURNS MALSUM

FOURTH TALE

GLOOSKAP AND THE WICKED WINPI [1]

I. WINPI STEALS GLOOSKAP'S FAMILY

GLOOSKAP built him a wigwam. He covered it with bark sewed in wide strips.[2] These strips he could roll up and load in his canoe, when he wanted to move his lodge to a new place.

He pitched his tent near the sea. It was a good place for a camp.

Every day, Glooskap went out hunting, and the little marten fished along the shore; and neither came home empty-handed.

One day as he came in from his hunt, Glooskap saw that no smoke was rising from his wigwam. "That is strange!" he thought.

[1] Wĭ́n - pĭ   [2] See Note 6.

143

He dropped his pack and raised the door skin. There was no one within.

"My grandmother is stolen!" cried Glooskap.

Swiftly he ran around the wigwam. On the side nearest the sea were tracks.

He followed them; they led to the beach. There he saw what sad misfortune had overtaken his family.

Putting out from shore in a canoe was Winpi, a sorcerer, Glooskap's enemy. Winpi's wife and babe were with him.

In the stern sat Glooskap's grandmother and Abistanooch; the grandmother was weeping.

Glooskap strode angrily to the water's edge.

"Wicked Winpi," he shouted, "bring back my grandmother and my younger brother!"

But Winpi paid no heed to his words. He swung his canoe around and headed out to sea.

Glooskap had two wonderful dogs.[1] One was white, the other

[1] See Note 7.

144

black; and they could grow small or big, as Glooskap bade them.

Winpi had stolen these dogs, and they were with him in the canoe. They heard Glooskap's voice and began to bark.

"Grandmother," shouted Glooskap, "send me back my dogs!"

The grandmother stopped weeping. A wooden platter lay in the bottom of the canoe[1]; into this she put the dogs, no bigger than mice, and set the platter on the water.

The platter floated to land and Glooskap took it up.

[1] See Note 8.

II. Glooskap sets off to seek Winpi

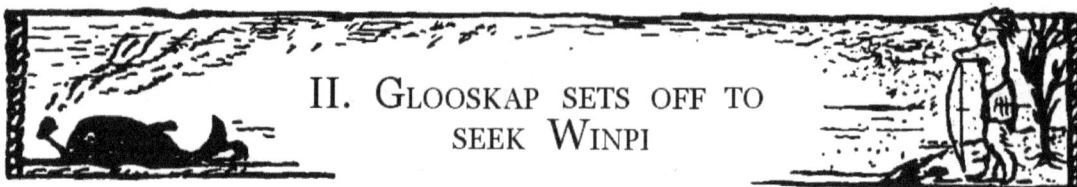

Glooskap rested seven years before he followed Winpi. Why he waited, no one knows. It may be he did so to gain power.[1] To fight Winpi, he knew, was no child's play.

At the end of seven years, Glooskap took his bow, hid his dogs under his coat, and set forth; but he paused, and leaned a stick against his door. "Strangers will see the stick," he thought, "and know that no one is within."

He went down to the beach and sang a song that the whales obey. A small black whale arose and came swimming in to land.

Glooskap tried the whale's back with his foot. The whale sank; Glooskap sent him away.

Again he sang, and a great she whale arose in the ocean. She was Bootup,[2] hugest of all whales. Slowly she swam to shore. Glooskap leaped and stood upon her back.

"Whither shall I take you, grandson?" asked the whale.

"Along the coast; I seek Winpi!" answered Glooskap.

Bootup headed to sea, and for hours bore the chief over the waves. Toward mid-afternoon, Glooskap wanted to land.

"Grandmother," he called, "turn in toward the beach. I want to go ashore!"

[1] See Note 9.   [2] Bŏŏt - ŭp

146

Bootup obeyed, but feared the shoals lying along the coast. She called to Glooskap, "Grandson, do you see land lying near?"

"No," he answered, "I see only deep water!"

After a time the water grew shoal. Bootup saw, below, the white shells of the clams and cried in fear, "Grandson, do you not see the land stretching out like a bowstring?"

"No," he answered, "we are yet far from land."

The water grew more shoal. Bootup could even hear the clams singing. She asked Glooskap, "Grandson, what are they singing?"

He answered her in a song:

> "They tell you to hurry, to hurry,
> To hurry me on
> O'er the water, the water,
> As fast as you can!"

The song shamed Bootup, and she rushed through the water at the top of her speed. Suddenly she ran aground. Glooskap sprang safely to land; but the whale lay stranded with her big head high on the beach.

Tears came into Bootup's eyes. Sobbing, she sang:

"Alas, grandson,

You would be my death!

I cannot leave the land;

I shall swim the sea no more!"

Glooskap laughed and again answered in a song:

"Nay, grandmother, have no fear!
You shall swim the sea once more!"

And with a push of his mighty bow, he sent the whale off into deep water.

Bootup dived, but came up again, blowing gladly. Once more she swam near to shore. "Grandson," she called, "have you a pipe and tobacco?"

Glooskap lighted a short pipe, and put it in her mouth. The whale swam away, smoking as she went.

To this day when a whale blows, the Indians say, "She is smoking Glooskap's Pipe!"[1]

[1] See Note 10.

BOOTUP SMOKING GLOOSKAP'S PIPE

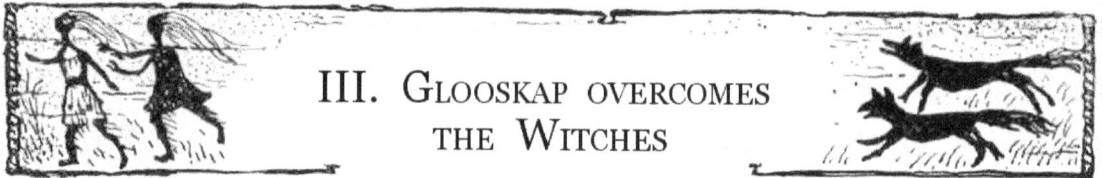

III. Glooskap overcomes the Witches

Glooskap went on afoot, and soon came to the ashes of a dead campfire. There were tracks about, and in the sand lay a broken birch dish. Glooskap picked it up; it was the marten's.

"Winpi camped here three months ago," thought Glooskap. He dropped the dish. "It shall go hard with Winpi when I find him!" he cried.

He went on. One day he came to a low hut. An old woman, ugly and in rags, sat within by a fire of sticks. She was a witch.

She tried to look pleased when she saw Glooskap. "Come in!" she said. She begged Glooskap to fetch her some firewood.[1]

Glooskap took her packing strap and fetched in a great load of sticks on his back.

[1] See Note 11.

150

The witch heaped the sticks on the fire and warmed Glooskap some broth.[1]   He ate, and she sat by the fire, nodding; the smoke made her sleepy.

Glooskap put down the bowl, empty.   The witch opened her eyes. "Grandson," she cried, "things creep in my hair!" She bent her head; Glooskap was astonished to see that her hair was full of live toads.

"Kill them!" cried the witch.

Glooskap would not do this, for he knew the toads' poison would enter his skin. He took them out and put them, one by one, under the empty bowl. The witch fell asleep.

She awoke to find Glooskap gone. Her fire had died. The toads had overturned the bowl and were hopping out of the door.

The witch sprang up in a rage. "Glooskap mocks me!" she cried; and she rushed from the lodge.

Glooskap saw her coming. He took out his dogs and put them on the ground, whispering, "Grow big!"

The dogs grew to great size and slew the witch.

[1] See Note 12.

Glooskap came next to a narrow pass between hills. Standing in the pass were two giant dogs baying savagely.

Glooskap put his own little dogs upon the ground. They, growing to great size, flew at the strange dogs and tore them into bits.

Farther on, Glooskap saw a tall wigwam with smoke curling upward. "An enemy is there!" he thought.

He made his way to the wigwam and found an old man, with two grown-up daughters. The old man was a boöoin.[1]

The boöoin's daughters came out, saucily tossing their hair and laughing. They had strings of sausages on their arms.

These sausages are made of bears' entrails, smoked, with the fat turned in. Indian girls think them a fit gift for their lovers.

The two girls tried to throw the sausages over Glooskap's neck. "We make you a gift!" they cried.

[1] Bōō - ṓ - ĭn   See Note 13.

The sausages were bewitched. Had they fallen on Glooskap they would have held him fast.

Glooskap answered not a word, but took out his dogs. "Grow big!" he whispered to them.

He had taught his dogs, when he bade them be quiet, they should fight. When now they began to growl, Glooskap cried, "*Kuss!*[1] — Stop!" This the dogs knew as "Seek, seek them!" They flew at the girls, who rose in their true shape, ugly witches.

There was an awful battle. The barking of the dogs and the witches' screams were like the noise of a storm. And all the time Glooskap was calling, "*Kuss, kuss!* — Stop, stop!" At last the witches fled.

Glooskap entered the wigwam. He found the father sitting with the kettle ready; for booöins eat human flesh.

Glooskap scornfully threw over him the magic sausages. "Eat these!" he cried.

Caught in his own sausages, the booöin fell helpless; and Glooskap slew him.

[1] Kūss

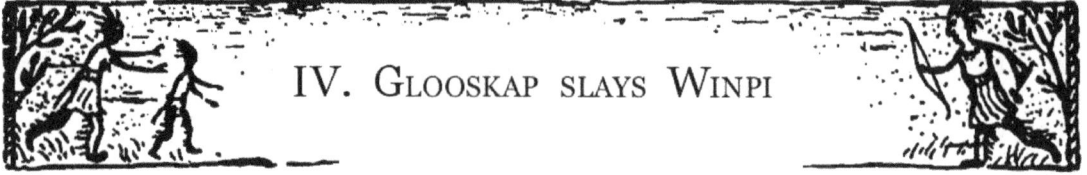

IV. Glooskap slays Winpi

Glooskap went on, meeting no more foes. The way led him again to the sea. Far out he saw an island. "Winpi hides there," he thought.

Once more he sang the whale's song. A black whale arose and bore him to the island.

Hardly had he landed when he found remains of a forsaken camp. Tracks, still fresh, were in the sand; and in the ashes of the fire a few coals were yet burning. A new birch dish lay on the ground. It was the marten's; and marks scratched upon it told Glooskap all he needed to know.[1]

"Winpi camped here last night," he thought.

He hastened on, following the campers' trail. The way led him into the island. Toward evening, he saw the light of a camp fire.

He was nearing the camp, when he heard the sound of a stick breaking. Softly he stole through the trees and looked.

[1] See Note 14.

154

here was Abistanooch, gathering wood; he looked starved, but his clothes were good.[1]

"Younger brother!" Glooskap called softly.

Abistanooch did not hear. Smiling, Glooskap threw a chip; it fell at the marten's feet.

Abistanooch looked up. "A squirrel did it!" he thought; and he went on gathering wood.

Glooskap called again. The marten looked up, and saw him; he was beside himself for joy.

"Quiet little brother!" said Glooskap.

Abistanooch told him all that Winpi did; how the Bear Woman had to scour pots while the marten fetched wood and cared for Winpi's babe.

Abistanooch wept as he told this. He was ashamed to be a servant and do woman's work.

Glooskap heard him and said: "Take your wood to camp. Winpi will ask you for a drink. Fetch muddy water and give to him. Then run hither!"

[1] See Note 15.

155

Abistanooch stooped and lifted his load. "I will do as you bid me!" he said. All happened as Glooskap said. Winpi asked for a drink. Abistanooch fetched him a cup of foulest water. Winpi tasted it.

"*Uk, say!*[1] — Oh, dreadful!" he cried. "Fetch me clean water!"

Abistanooch threw the cup in his face. Winpi sprang to his feet; but the little marten ran for the trees where Glooskap was hiding.

"Help! elder brother!" he cried; he could hear Winpi coming.

"Your brother is far away!" cried Winpi; but even as he spoke, Glooskap stood before them. Winpi fell back, afraid. Then calling up all his power, he rose a great giant, until he stood above the tallest trees.

Glooskap laughed aloud. "Behold!" he cried, and he began to grow. Taller he rose, and taller, until his head touched the clouds.

"I am undone!" cried Winpi; and he covered his face.

Glooskap reached down with his bow and tapped Winpi on the shoulders, as he would a little dog. Winpi fell dead.

Glooskap went into the wigwam where Winpi's wife sat, crying out with fear; but all he said was, "Begone!" She took her babe and gladly went away.

[1] Ük - sāy

156

FIFTH TALE

GLOOSKAP AND THE FRIENDLY LOONS

WHEN Glooskap was seeking Winpi, he came one day to a lake. He was standing, gazing at the water, when the sound of wings made him look up. A bird flew by, circled around the lake, and again passed Glooskap. As the bird flew by a third time, Glooskap called, "What do you want?"

"To be your servant!" said the bird. He told Glooskap his name was Kwemoo[1] and that he was chief of the loons.

Afterwards, on Winpi's island, Glooskap came upon a town of many lodges.[2] It was the loons' village. The island was their home.

[1] Kwé - moo   [2] See Note 16.

157

Chief Kwemoo and his people gladly welcomed Glooskap. They feasted him many days, dancing each night in the town lodge. The young men of the village gave him rich gifts.

Glooskap was pleased with the loons. He made them his messengers; and ever afterwards they were his faithful friends.

He taught them a long, wild cry, like the howl of a wolf. "When you have need," he said, "make that cry, and I will come."

Whenever the Indians hear a loon cry, they say, "Kwemoo is calling Glooskap!"

GLOOSKAP'S MESSENGER

F.N.Wilson

SIXTH TALE

MIKCHICH,[1] GLOOSKAP'S UNCLE

I. Mikchich wins a Wife

GLOOSKAP did not call Bootup to take him from the island. He built a canoe and, with his family, paddled to the mainland.

He landed at a place called Piktook,[2] or Bubbling Air, from air bubbles that rise in the water. A village was there of more than a hundred wigwams.

Here Glooskap left his family. "I am going into the village," he told them. Abistanooch took the paddle and, with the old grandmother, went on down the coast.

---

[1] Mĭk´- chĭch   [2] Pĭ́k - tōok

159

On the side of the village nearest the water stood a small, ill-built wigwam with a squat roof. There lived in it a man with withered face, old and ugly.

He was Mikchich, the turtle, and he dwelt alone. No one wanted him for a husband. "He is so ugly! —we cannot bear to look at him!" the village maidens said.

When an Indian comes to a strange town, he stops always at the first lodge he finds. So it was that Glooskap, coming up from the beach, stopped at Mikchich's door. He pushed the door-skin aside, and entered.

Mikchich looked up. His old face puckered into a smile, and he took his pipe from his mouth.

"Kwai!" [1] he cried, "Welcome! Come and sit back of the fire." [2] He dragged out a rush mat for Glooskap to sit upon.

When they had smoked, Mikchich brought out dried moose meat and fat of bears' entrails. "We will feast, nephew!" he said; for Mikchich wished well to everybody, and thought nothing better than to have Glooskap call him uncle.

It was soon noised that a handsome stranger had come to Mikchich's wigwam. All were eager to see him, but Glooskap did

[1] Kwaī   [2] See Note 17.

160

not go to the village feasts. He liked to stay in the lodge and watch his uncle's quaint ways and hear his stories.

A great feast was to be made, with games and dances. The villagers sent a crier to invite Glooskap.

"Go, nephew," said his uncle, "or they will think you fear to enter the games!"

Glooskap laughed. "Why not go yourself, uncle?" he asked. "It will be good to see the games. And the village maidens will be there! You should think of winning you a wife."

Mikchich sighed, and thrust the ashes from his pipe. He filled the bowl and held the stem to Glooskap.

"Nephew," he said, "I am old and have little wit. And I am ugly so that young women shun me. Better for me that I eat alone!"

Glooskap sat, blowing little clouds from his nostrils.

"Uncle," he said. "let me see if I cannot make you young!"

The day of the feast came. Glooskap took off his belt and gave it to Mikchich.

"Put on this belt, uncle!" he said. Mikchich did so. The wrinkles faded from his old face. His fat ankles grew slender. He became young again, and handsome.

Glooskap lent him his own robe and leggings.

"There, uncle," he said, "let us see what they will think of you!"

Mikchich came to the feast, and all wondered to see so handsome a man. None leaped so nimbly, or ran so swiftly, in the games.

Sitting with the women, watching the games, were the three bright-eyed daughters of the chief. The youngest, Mikchich thought, was the prettiest. He could hardly keep his eyes from her.

At night, when he came home, he said to Glooskap, "Nephew, I have seen the maiden I want, but I fear she will not wed an old man like me!"

Glooskap smiled. "We shall see, uncle!" he said.

The next morning, Glooskap laid a great belt of wampum beads on his arm[1] and went to the chief's wigwam. He threw the belt at the chief's feet.

"My uncle, Mikchich, tires of dwelling alone!" he said.

The chief sat, thoughtful. He called his wife. "Shall we give our daughter to Mikchich?" he asked.

"Yes," she answered.

The chief called his youngest daughter to him. "Cook venison," he said. "Fetch boughs for your husband to sit upon."

This she did. While the venison boiled, she gathered hemlock boughs and covered them with a skin, for a couch. When all was ready, she went to Mikchich's lodge and said, "I have come for you!"

Mikchich arose and went with her to the chief's wigwam. He sat on the couch, and the maiden gave him venison to eat. And so they were wed.

[1] See Note 18.

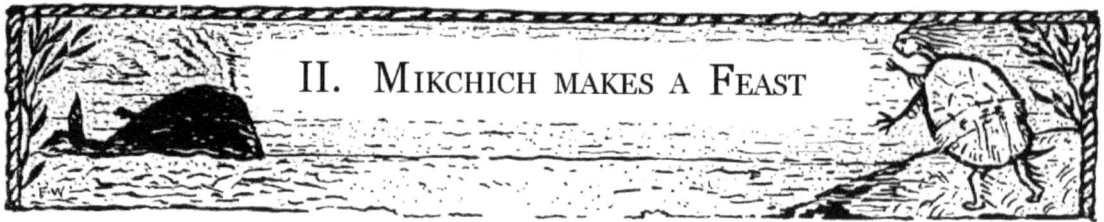

II. Mikchich makes a Feast

Mikchich wanted to give a feast. "It is for my wedding," he told Glooskap.

"Make it a big feast, uncle," his nephew said; and to this end he gave Mikchich great power.

"Go down to the rocks, by the sea," Glooskap bade him. "There you will see a number of whales swimming. Catch one of them, and fetch it hither; but do not bring it farther than the sand heap before your door!"

All this Mikchich did, for Glooskap's belt gave him strength. He caught a fat whale by the tail, and drew it, struggling and bellowing, from the water. The villagers were astonished to see him come back with the whale, still struggling, on his back.

Mikchich was much puffed up to see that all had their eyes upon him. He forgot Glooskap's warning.

"The whale is not heavy," he thought; "I will take it into my wigwam!" But when he came to the sand heap, he stumbled; and the whale, falling on him, crushed him flat.

The villagers ran and rolled the whale off Mikchich. "He is dead!" they cried. They told Glooskap.

Glooskap laughed. "Cut up the whale," he said. "Mikchich will live!"

They cut up the whale as they were directed, and made ready the feast; and they were sitting down to eat, when in came Mikchich, none the worse for having been dead.

"I have slept!" he said; and he stretched his legs and yawned.

After this the villagers feared Glooskap.

The turtle's shell is still flat, where the whale crushed it.

III. Mikchich is Smoked

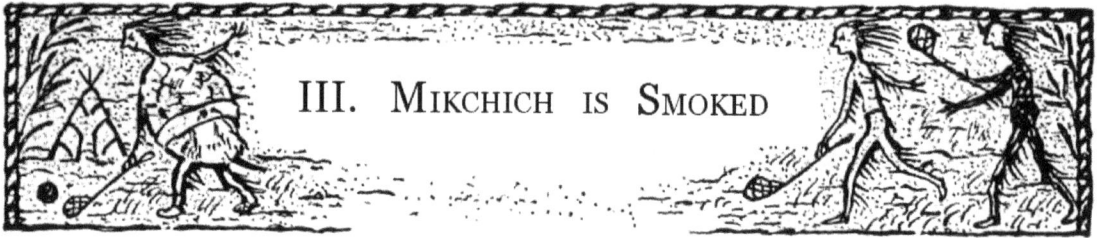

The young men of the village took it ill that Mikchich had wed the chief's daughter. "Ugly, lazy man!" they said. "We thought one of us should win her." They talked of it until they hated Mikchich; and they plotted to kill him.

Mikchich lived with his wife, in her father's lodge. Glooskap came to him.

"Uncle," he said, "the young men plan to kill you!"

"How will they kill me?" Mikchich asked.

"They will ask you to play a game of ball,"[1] said Glooskap. "The ball will be rolled toward your father-in-law's lodge; as you run to catch it up, the players will try to trample you. They seek to slay you before your door!"

Mikchich sat, thoughtful. "What shall I do, nephew?" he asked.

"Wear my belt," said Glooskap. "It will give you power to leap over the wigwam. Twice you will leap safely. The third time you will be caught on the poles!"

All happened as he said. The young men asked Mikchich to a

[1] See Note 19.

game of ball. The ball rolled toward his lodge, and Mikchich ran to get it, when the players crowded upon him to trample him; but Mikchich made a leap and sailed high over the wigwam. He came down safely.

Again the ball rolled toward his lodge; and again Mikchich went sailing over the wigwam.

The third time he fell short. The poles caught him and he hung dangling over the smoke hole.

Much frightened, he looked down and saw Glooskap sitting inside. "Help, nephew," he cried. "Take me down!"

"Nay, Uncle," answered Glooskap, "you must hang in the smoke.[1] It will make you tough!" And he heaped fir branches on the fire, making a great smoke.

Mikchich was nigh strangled.

[1] See Note 20.

"Nephew," he cried, "you will kill me!"

He coughed and choked with the hot smoke.

"It is for your good," said Glooskap. "Hereafter you may go through flame, and it will not hurt you. You may live on land or in water. And you may go a long time without eating!"

When Mikchich was nearly dead with the smoke, Glooskap took him down. The turtle's skin had been made hard and brown by the smoke.

When Mikchich got his breath again, he thanked Glooskap.

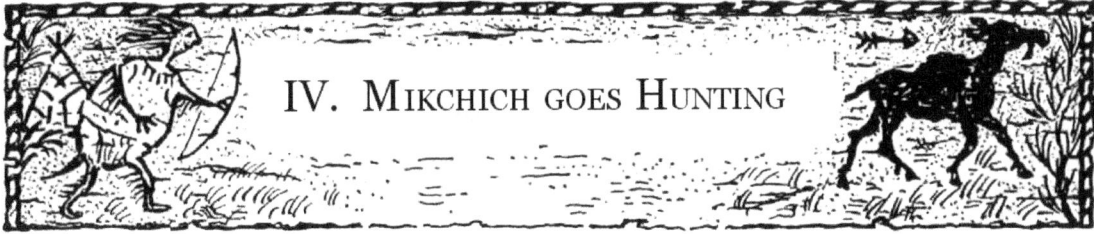

IV. MIKCHICH GOES HUNTING

But for all his skin was so tough, and he had a wife, Mikchich could not forget his old ways. He was still lazy, wishing well to everybody.

Autumn came. The men of the village were hunting, while the women dried meat[1] and stored it by for winter; but lazy Mikchich sat by his fire and smoked.

With the first snow, there was feasting and merry-making in the village; but in Mikchich's lodge was nothing to eat.

His wife was in a rage. "Lazy man," she cried, "the young men hunt to-day. Go you and kill us meat, before we starve!"

Mikchich arose with a sigh. He put on his snowshoes and started off after the hunters; but he was so awkward that he tripped and fell in the snow.

His wife was watching him from the wigwam door. "Awkward man!" she cried.

She went into the wigwam. "My husband," she said to her mother, "is lazy; and he is so awkward that he trips on his snowshoes!"

Her mother remembered how Mikchich leaped over the wigwam. "Wait, daughter," she said.

[1] See Note 21.

169

The young men, looking back, saw Mikchich stumble. They laughed to see his fat body roll in the snow.

"Awkward Mikchich!" they cried. "He is fat because he is lazy!" They went on, leaving him behind.

Mikchich struggled through the snow, puffing and blowing, but could not overtake the hunters. They disappeared in the forest.

But Mikchich was stout hearted. He bethought him of his flight over the wigwam. "I have on my nephew's belt," he said to himself.

He bent his legs, made a leap, and went sailing high over the heads of the others. They were laughing and telling one another of Mikchich, and did not see him.

Mikchich came down far away in the forest. He found tracks in the snow, followed them, and soon came upon a fat cow moose.[1]

[1] See Note 22.

He killed her and dragged the carcass to a path where the hunters must pass.

After a time the others came up. They saw Mikchich sitting on the dead moose, smoking his pipe. "I have waited for you!" he said gravely.

V. Mikchich Goes Through Fire and Water

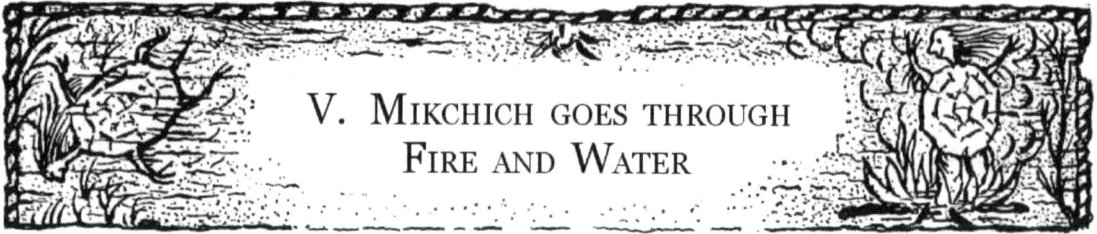

The time came when Glooskap had to leave Mikchich.

"I go, uncle," he said, "to my family. When I am gone, the young men will try again to slay you; but I think since you hung in the smoke, they will find it a hard thing to do!"

As Glooskap said, no sooner was he gone than the young men began to think how they might kill Mikchich. "Glooskap," they said, "cannot help him now!" Again they plotted to slay him.

They fetched wood, and when night came, they made a great fire at one end of the village. They hid by Mikchich's door; and in the morning when he came out, they seized him and dragged him to the fire. "We are going to burn you!" they cried.

Mikchich said nothing. "The fire," he thought, "cannot be hotter than when my nephew smoked me!" He had on Glooskap's belt.

With much straining, the young men lifted the turtle to their shoulders and heaved him into the fire. He fell in the coals, on his back.

172

Red sparks flew up. Then the flames closed over Mikchich and hid him.

But Mikchich was not dead. It was good, he found, to lie in the warm ashes. "They make a soft bed!" he thought.

He drew in his legs and hid his head in his shell. He yawned and closed his eyes.

The fire burned all that day and into the night. The young men were in high glee. All night they danced by the firelight,[1] singing:

"Mikchich is dead, is dead!"

Toward morning the flames died down. The young men were making ready to go when they heard a voice calling them. It was Mikchich. He had waked and was sitting in the ashes, shivering.

"I am cold!" he cried. "Heap wood on the fire!"

The young men were in a rage. "If you will not burn," they cried, "you shall drown!" They dragged the turtle out of the ashes and rolled him, like a stone, to the sea.

Morning had come. It was growing light. Mikchich struggled hard. "Do not drown me!" he cried. "Burn me, — do not drown me!" He dragged up rocks and tore bark from the tree with his feet.

[1] See Note 23.

The young men laughed aloud. "Mikchich is afraid!" they cried.

They tumbled him into a canoe and paddled out to deep water. There they dropped him overboard.

Slowly the turtle sank from sight. The young men waited; a few bubbles rose on the water.

"He is dead!" said they; and they paddled back to shore.

Day came; and at noon, a hot sun was shining. Some villagers were walking on the beach, talking of Mikchich's drowning.

"What is that?" asked one suddenly.

The others looked. On a rock that rose out of the water, lay something round like a muddy stone.

Two men got into a canoe and paddled out to the rock. There they saw Mikchich sunning himself.

The turtle raised his head. "Good-by!" he called. And he plumped off into the water.

MIKCHICH THE TURTLE

SEVENTH TALE

GLOOSKAP AND KITPOOSAGUNO[1]

GLOOSKAP overtook his family not many days after he left Mikchich. The marten had made a camp on the beach. He had dragged the canoe out of the water and turned it over for a shelter.

A fire burned on the sand. The old grandmother was broiling fish on the coals.

The little marten welcomed Glooskap. "I am glad you have come, elder brother," he said. "It is hard for me to steer the canoe alone!"

The next morning Glooskap and Abistanooch dragged the canoe to water. All got in; Glooskap pushed off.

[1] Kĭt - po͞os - ă - gŭn - ō

175

"Whither do we go?" asked his old grandmother.

"To visit Kitpoosaguno, on his island," answered Glooskap.

A gale was blowing, but Glooskap paddled, and the canoe rode the sea like a feather. The pitching of the boat made the old Bear Woman drowsy; and she curled up in the stern and went to sleep. Glooskap could hear her snore above the noise of the wind.

The sun was setting when the island rose in sight. It was high and rocky; but on one side was a bay, shut in between cliffs. Thither Glooskap steered, into smooth water.

"Awake, grandmother," he cried as he sprang ashore.

Kitpoosaguno heard the voices and came hastening down the beach.

"Kwai!" he roared, "Welcome, friends! Come to my wigwam. Come and we will feast!"

Kitpoosaguno was a giant, and his wigwam was like a mountain. He was Glooskap's friend. Both made war on the kookwesses[1] who had slain the good giant's mother.

Kitpoosaguno led his friends into his wigwam. All that evening they feasted, and into the night. In the morning the giant set his pot a-boiling, and they feasted again. When night fell, the giant said, "Let us go on the sea and spear fish by torchlight!"

"Shall we spear salmon?" asked Glooskap.

"Nay!" roared the giant. "Let us spear whales!"

"It is good sport," laughed Glooskap.

The giant lighted a torch of pitch and led the way to the beach.

In the sand near the water lay a large rock. The giant stooped and felt of it with his hands.

"This shall be our boat!" he roared. He lifted the rock to his head; it became a canoe.

[1] kŏŏk - wĕss - ĕş

177

By the torch's light he found a long, flat stone; and it became a paddle. With a round stone for a hammer, he struck a splinter from the edge of the cliff; and it became a spear.

The giant put the canoe from his head and pushed it out into the water.

"Who will take the paddle?" he asked.

"I!" said Glooskap.

"I will take the spear!" laughed the giant.

They stepped aboard. As they stood, side by side in the torchlight, Glooskap seemed almost as tall as the giant.

Kitpoosaguno bound the torch to the bow of the canoe. He took his spear, ready to strike.

Glooskap dipped his paddle; the canoe swung away.

A shield of bark was put over the torch, that its flame might not blind the giant's eyes. By the light that fell on the water, the two men could see the fish swimming in the bottom of the sea.

They had not been out long, when they passed a huge black

mass that moved. It was a great whale.

Kitpoosaguno hurled his spear. "A strike," he roared, "a strike!"

He caught the handle as it came up and raised the whale aloft, whirling it above his head like a minnow. The whale bellowed and squirmed upon the spear.

"Good fishing!" the giant roared.

He drew the whale off the point of his spear and tossed it into the canoe. The whale struggled, beating and lashing with its tail. The giant roared with delight.

Glooskap steered to shore. The giant shouldered the dead whale and sprang out on the sand. He led the way to his wigwam; Glooskap followed with the torch.

Kitpoosaguno spitted the whale over the fire to roast. His spit was a pine tree, lopped of branches.

When the meat steamed, the giant took the whale from the spit. "Your knife!" he said.

Glooskap handed him his stone knife; and the giant split the steaming whale in twain.

"A good feast!" he roared; and he and Glooskap ate the whale between them.

Kitpoosaguno, his stomach filled, was full of frolic. He went to the door, raised the skin, and put out his head. Twilight had faded, but there was a little red in the sky. The giant came back.

"The sky is red!" he roared. "We shall have cold to-night!" He looked at his friend, and laughed.

Glooskap knew what he meant. Kitpoosaguno was going to bring cold by magic.

"Let us have a good fire!" Glooskap said, smiling.

Then he bade Abistanooch fetch in wood for the fire. The marten did so, until he had a heap higher than a tree, beside the door.

The giant had killed a porpoise the day before; and he had tried out the oil into two great kettles, that stood by the door.

"Pour the oil on the wood; it will make it burn!" roared the giant; he was full of glee.

The marten emptied the kettles over the wood. He heaped sticks on the fire, and the flames went roaring upward to the smoke hole. Glooskap and the giant sat, smoking and telling tales.[1]

The fire gave little heat. The oil burned fiercely, but icy air came rushing down the smoke hole. Abistanooch and the old grandmother sat shivering.

At midnight the fire burned down. The marten froze to death. The old grandmother groaned, sank on the floor, and died. The wigwam poles cracked, and rocks split with the frost.

Glooskap and the giant talked on.

The sun rose on the morrow, yellow and shining. The giant yawned; he thrust the ashes from his pipe and rose to his feet.

Glooskap went to where the martin lay. "Up, little brother," he called. "Awake, grandmother!"

The old Bear Woman arose and put the pot on the fire for breakfast.

The pot boiled, the meal was eaten, and the giant took down his bow.

"Let us go hunting!" he roared. He strode from the wigwam; Glooskap followed him.

The game, that day, seemed to know Glooskap and the giant were out hunting. Flocks of ducks rose from the lakes and flew away. The deer fled into the forest.

The hunters got only a small beaver that Glooskap killed.

They skinned the beaver, and the giant tied its pelt to his

[1] See Note 24.

garter; it hung dangling at his knee, like a mouse skin. As the giant walked, the pelt grew and grew, until it broke away by its weight.

"It is a big skin!" roared the giant, laughing.

He twisted a sapling into a withe and tied the pelt to his waist. Still the skin grew, until it tore a road-way through the forest, uprooting trees in its path.

The hunters reached home at nightfall. They put out in their canoe and again speared whales. As they came in from their fishing, Glooskap said: "The sky is red. I think we shall have cold to-night!"

The giant understood. "Good!" he roared; and his laugh shook the cliffs.

They returned to the wigwam. Again the marten brought in wood. The old grandmother even fetched skins for the men to wrap them in.

It was colder this time. Before midnight the fire had burned

out. Soon the little marten died. The old grandmother lay on her back with her eyes shut, frozen. Even the giant shivered under his robe.

Glooskap talked on, caring nothing for the cold.

Morning came at last. Glooskap brought the marten and the old Bear Woman back to life, took leave of the good giant, and went away.

EIGHTH TALE

THE LITTLE LADS AND THE KOOKWESSES

THE kookwesses that slew Kitpoosaguno's mother were giants. They were a wicked folk. Their bodies were covered with hair, and they hunted men; but they had not much wit.

When Glooskap was on Kitpoosaguno's island, a thing happened that made a great noise in the land.

Some little lads had gone out to hunt birds. A kookwess saw the boys. "They are fat!" he thought; "I will call them to me." He began to drum on his breast like a cock partridge.

The lads heard the drumming. "A partridge!" they cried; and

184

they stole through the forest with arrows drawn.

The kookwess was hidden in a hollow. The boys were almost upon him when the giant rose, caught the lads and dropped them, one by one, upon a stone, to kill them.

The giant had none too much wit. What he thought was a stone was an ant hill. The boys were only stunned.

The kookwess tossed the lads into the boochkajoo,[1] or bark basket on his back, and started home. The jolting of the basket brought the boys out of their swoon. They sat up. One began to weep.

"Do not weep!" said the eldest. "Let us try to get out of the basket!"

They drew together, talking in whispers.

One of the boys had a knife. "Let us cut a hole in the basket," he said.

"Good!" said the eldest. "But do not let the kookwess hear us!"

They waited until the giant was passing through the thickest part of the forest. The scraping of the basket against the tree tops

---

[1] booch - ka - joo.   See Note 25.

drowned the noise of the knife.

The boys soon cut a hole big enough. One by one, they dropped to the ground. The last eldest dropped last.

The giant was so strong that he did not feel how light the basket had become.

When he got home, he put down the basket by his door, and went in. An older kook-wess was sitting by the fire.

"Father," said the other, "I bring game to-day!"

The elder giant got up, and both went outside. They raised the lid of the basket. The boys were gone!

The younger giant made a great howl. "We shall go to bed hungry!" he bawled.

His father led him into the wigwam. "We have a little meat, son," he said. He raked coals out of the ashes and spitted the meat, to roast it.

The lads meanwhile had reached home. Their story made a great stir in the village.

Friends and kinsmen caught up bows and ran to the hollow

where the giant had hidden. They followed his trail by the trees broken down in his path.

They reached the giants' wigwam at sundown. Through cracks in the bark roof, they saw the two giants sitting, waiting for their meal to cook.

Pitt!— an arrow came flitting through the bark covering of the wigwam. It struck the kookwess who had carried off the children.

He put up his hand and felt his side. "It hurts me here!" he said. He thought he had a stitch.

But *pitt!*—another arrow struck him, and another. The kookwess slipped down on the floor. His eyes closed.

"Do you sleep, son?" the elder asked.

As he spoke, *pitt!*—an arrow struck him also. A sharp pain went through him. His head swam. He fell over on his side.

The Indians rushed in. The two giants were dead.

THE INDIANS RUSHED IN

NINTH TALE

GLOOSKAP AND THE WITCHES

SOME of the forest folk envied Glooskap, and about this time rose up against him. "Why should we obey Glooskap?" they asked. They forgot the many times he had come to their help.

A council was called. Runners were sent throughout the land, and the people came flocking in from every part.

They met in a long lodge.[1] The old men and warriors sat in the back; the women and children, on the left of the door.

Some have it that Mikchich was chief of the council; but this is not true. Mikchich loved his nephew and was faithful to him while he lived.

[1] See note 26.

188

The people feasted, and there was much speaking. Some cried, "We will slay Glooskap!" Others said, "No, let us put him down from being our chief!" Few had any good to say of him.

Glooskap knew all that was going on. He smiled that any should think to slay him.

The third day of the council, a strange old woman came into the lodge. She was bent, and walked with a stick; and her thin, gray hair fell in her eyes.

It was Glooskap dressed in his grandmother's skirt, with his hair falling loose.

No one offered the stranger a seat. She came and sat down between two witches, the Toad Woman and the Porcupine Woman; they were listening to the speeches.[1]

The stranger sat awhile, silent. At last she asked humbly, "You think to slay Glooskap; but will that be easy to do?"

The witches were angered that the stranger should speak to them. They scowled at her.

[1] See Note 27.

"What is that to you?" said the Toad Woman, rudely.

The stranger shrunk back. "I meant no harm," she said softly.

Presently she arose. Leaning on her stick, she gently touched the tips of the witches' noses. Then she went away.

The speaking ended. The two witches looked up; and each saw that the other's nose was gone.

Screaming in terror, they rushed out and ran to a pool. They bent over the water and looked. Their noses were flat!

So it came that the toad and the porcupine lost their noses; and they have none to this day!

THEIR NOSES WERE FLAT

F.N.WILSON.

TENTH TALE

GLOOSKAP AND POKINSKWESS

AFTER this, Glooskap went to live with a village of Indians called Pogumks,[1] or Fishers. The villagers welcomed him. "You bring us luck," they said. "Our nets never brought up so many fish!" They even made him their chief.

But there was one in the village who spoke no good of Glooskap. This was Pokinskwess[2]; and he was full of envy because he wanted to be chief himself. He thought long how he might slay Glooskap or put him out of the village.

Spring came, and the villagers were making ready to move camp. All was bustle and noise among the wigwams. Dogs were

---

[1] Pṓ - gŭmks   [2] Pŏk´ - ĭn - skwĕss

191

yelping. Children were running about. The women were rolling up the bark coverings of their lodges to load upon their backs.

Pokinskwess came to Glooskap. "The camp is not yet ready to march," he said. "Let us go to yonder island and gather gulls' eggs." He pointed to an island off the coast.

Glooskap was willing. He went down to the beach with Pokinskwess, and they launched a canoe. Glooskap held the boat while Pokinskwess got in. They paddled to the island.

There was no beach to land upon. The island was but a rocky cliff, rising in the water. The gulls' nests were in clefts of the rock overhead.

Many of the gulls had young, and were bringing them food. Pokinskwess brought his canoe around to the foot of the cliff.

"Who shall climb for the eggs?" he asked.

"I," said Glooskap.

"I will stay to guard the canoe," said Pokinskwess.

Glooskap climbed up the cliff. He had a basket on his back, and into it he put the eggs. The gulls flew about him in a white cloud. They made a great outcry.

Pokinskwess sat in the canoe, paddle in hand. When Glooskap was but a speck on the cliff, Pokinskwess softly stole away.

He reached home just as the villagers were setting off. They wondered why Glooskap did not come with them. Pokinskwess said nothing.

At night, the villagers made camp and awaited Glooskap. When he did not come, the old men made Pokinskwess chief in his stead.

Glooskap, meanwhile, could find no way to leave the island. But he did not fear; he had gulls'

eggs to eat, and in a hollow in the rocks he found rain water. He could not starve.

"The sea serpent will help me!" said Glooskap at last. And he began to sing:

"Sea serpent, grandfather under the ocean,

I, Glooskap, call you!"

The sea serpent was old and fat and lazy; and he lay asleep on the bottom of the ocean.

The song waked him; he raised his head.

"I thought I heard my grandson singing," he said.

He listened. Again he heard the song.

The old serpent wriggled his tail, and began to swim upward in the water. He came out not far from the island, and soon lay at the foot of the cliff, where the canoe had been.

"I am here, grandson!" he called.

Glooskap had his robe belted about him for the wind was chill upon the cliff. In the folds of his robe he made a pocket and dropped two round stones within. He climbed down the cliff and leaped astride the serpent's back.

"Take me to land, grandfather!" he cried.

The serpent bent his tail and went wriggling over the sea. But he was old and lazy. There had been a calm; now waves rolled, for Pokinskwess had raised a storm. It was hard for the serpent to swim. Slower he wriggled, and slower. He almost stopped.

Glooskap took a stone from the pocket of his robe. He threw it with all his strength, and *whack!*— it struck one of the serpent's yellow horns.

"Grandson," cried the sea serpent, "spare my horn!"

"Do not sleep, grandfather!" cried Glooskap, laughing.

The serpent wriggled on. But the waves were high, and the swimming was hard; and he had a longing to rest. He stretched out on the water, when *whack!*— a stone struck his other horn.

"Grandson," he cried again, "spare my horn!"

Glooskap laughed aloud. "Do not sleep, grandfather!" he cried.

At last they came to land. Glooskap sprang ashore, and the serpent dived to the bottom of the ocean.

Glooskap was soon at the place where the village had stood. Night was coming on; he crept under a shelter of branches and slept.

Early the next morning he found the villagers' trail and followed it. In a few days, he knew he was nearing their camp.

One afternoon, he overtook them on the march.

The very first one he saw was his old grandmother, hobbling along on a stick. She was lame and had fallen behind. On her back was Abistanooch, strapped in a cradle, like a babe.[1] They looked starved and weak.

From his place on her back, Abistanooch saw Glooskap coming through the trees, and cried out, "Grandmother, I see my elder brother!"

The old grandmother turned, but Glooskap had hid. "Foolish one," she cried. "Glooskap is not here!" Tears came into her eyes.

[1] See Note 28.

196

A little way on, Abistanooch cried again, "Grandmother, I see my brother!"

The old Bear Woman turned quickly and saw Glooskap. She cried out and danced for joy, dropping the little marten from her back. He crept from his cradle, and all stood and laughed.

Abistanooch told his brother all the evil Pokinskwess did him. "He makes me serve him," he said. "All night I care for his babe!"

Glooskap told him what he should do. "Go into camp," he said. "Build a hot fire of hemlock bark. Catch up Pokinskwess's babe and make as if you would throw it in the fire. Then run to me!"

All this the marten did. He caught up the babe, and Pokinskwess sprang at him in wrath.

Abistanooch fled. "Help, elder brother!" he cried.

"Glooskap cannot help you," cried Pokinskwess. Glooskap stepped from behind a tree. "I am here," he cried.

Fear came into Pokinskwess's eyes. "I but ran at Abistanooch in sport!" he said.

"I know you and your evil ways," cried Glooskap; and he hurled Pokinskwess with his back against a tree.

Pokinskwess stuck fast to the trunk. Glooskap and Abistanooch went on into the camp, laughing.

Pokinskwess carried a hatchet and wedge[1] in his belt. With these he set to cutting himself loose; and all that night they in camp could hear him pounding and chopping at the wood. In the morning they saw that he had a great lump of wood on his back.

[1] See Note 29.

All mocked him, and the women cried: "Pokinskwess forsook Glooskap; and now he has a lump of wood on his back!"

Pokinskwess fled, mad with shame. "Men mock me!" he said aloud. "Would I were something to bite and sting them forever!"

As he spoke, lo, he shrunk small as his own wicked soul! His mouth grew long, like a sting. His arms became wings. He became a mosquito, that bites and stings men. On the mosquito's back is a lump, like a wedge of wood.

ELEVENTH TALE

PULOWECH,[1] GLOOSKAP'S FRIEND

I. PULOWECH GETS HIM A WIFE

PULOWECH, the partridge, and his cousin Wejek[2] were hunters. They had a camp by a lake, where maple and ash trees grew. Pulowech was Glooskap's friend.

The cousins were not alike. Pulowech was slow to speak, and did nothing in a hurry. Wejek was younger; he had a good heart, but he was hasty.

One day in winter, Pulowech was walking by the lake. As he came around a rock, he saw three girls sitting by an air hole in the ice; they were braiding their hair and laughing.

[1] Pŭl´- lō - wĕch.   See Note 30.   [2] Wĕ́jĕk

200

Pulowech stood watching them. "They are water maidens," he thought, and a longing filled his soul. "I will steal one and have her for my wife," he said softly. "She shall keep my pot boiling for me!" And he stole over the ice toward the girls.

A hard snow lay on the ice. Pulowech was almost up to the girls when his foot crunched through the snow, making a noise. One of the maidens looked up.

"Oo !" she cried. "I see a man!" And all plumped head-first into the water.

Pulowech went slowly home. He could not put the youngest of the girls out of his mind. "Her teeth were like shells!" he thought; and he sighed.

But Pulowech was not a man who gave up easily.

He was up before daylight, and went again to the lake, where he gathered fir boughs and craftily strewed them about the shore. "The water maidens will think the wind blew them there," he said to himself.

He laid one bough far out on the ice; under it he crept and hid, waiting for morning.

The sun arose. Pulowech peeped out and saw the water in the hole all golden in the light.

Soon a pretty head popped up in the water, then another, and another; and three merry maidens, laughing, clambered up on the ice. They unbound and began to braid their hair.

Pulowech crept from under the fir bough and ran towards the maidens. Again, one hearing his steps, cried out, *"Oo!* I see a man!" And all went head-first under the ice.

But Pulowech did not go away empty-handed. In her haste, the youngest of the girls had dropped her hairstring, and it lay on the ice. Pulowech picked it up.

"She will come to me!" he thought. "Her life is in the string!"

In his wigwam, he tied the hairstring to the tent pole, above the place where he sat. He filled his pipe and waited.

In a little while there came footsteps. Gently the door-skin was pushed aside and the maiden entered. She saw the hairstring. Tears were in her eyes, but she smiled.

She went to the fire and knelt to stir the coals. Then she put water in the pot, and dried meat, and set it on the fire to boil.

Pulowech, watching her, smiled softly. He knew she would have him for her husband.

II. Booöins steal Pulowech's Wife

Booöins and witches were then in the land. Pulowech never left his wife alone, fearing they might find her and steal her from him.

But a time came when he had to leave her. Wejek was gone. There was little to eat in the wigwam, and Pulowech had to hunt or his wife would go hungry. He made ready to go.

"Open to no one," he told his wife, "after the sun sets. The booöins cannot enter while the door is fast!"

"I will not open," she said.

Pulowech started off. Before the sun went down, his wife fetched in a heap of wood for the night. She drew the door and made it fast with a thong.

She stirred up the fire, put on wood, and lay down. The blaze was warm and pleasant. It was cold outside.

At midnight a wind arose. The little wife awoke. There was a noise as of scraping at the door; she listened.

"Open!" said a voice.

"No," she answered bravely; but her heart beat fast.

And well might she be frightened. The voice was of an old boöin; he had come, with his friends, to take her.

The boöin changed his voice, speaking now like her sister, now like her brother, "Open, dear sister!"

She would not open.

Again the boöin changed his voice. The little wife thought that she heard her mother, then her old father, calling to her, "Open, daughter; I am weary and cold!"

Her heart ached. She ran to the door and untied the thong.

The old boöin sprang into the wigwam. "Take her!" he screamed; and his friends dragged her away into the forest.

Far off, they built a fire and fetched drums, and passed the night feasting and singing. When they departed, nothing was left of the little wife.

That same morning, Wejek came home. He wondered to see tracks about the door. He stooped and looked at them.

"They are boöins' tracks!" he cried.

He ran into the wigwam. It was empty.

"My cousin's wife is stolen!" cried Wejek; and he ran out, following the boöins' trail.

He overtook the boöins just as they were leaving their feast.

They fell upon him with cries. Wejek fought; but in the end, they slew him.

III. PULOWECH SLAYS THE BOOÖINS

THE evening of the same day, Pulowech came home loaded with venison. His heart sank when he found his wigwam empty.

"Wife, wife!" he called. There was no answer. Wejek's knife lay on the floor.

Pulowech did not act hastily. He made a fire, ate, and spread his robe to sleep; but before he lay down, he set a wooden bowl in the back of the wigwam and filled it with water.

In the morning when he looked, the bowl was full of blood; and Pulowech knew that his wife and cousin were slain.

"I will find them who did it!" he cried, as he caught up his bow and hatchet.

The booöins' tracks were not new, but nothing escaped Pulowech's eyes; he followed the trail, unwearied.

He had not gone many days, when he came to a cliff over-hanging the way. He was passing under, when he looked up and saw a man's knee sticking out of the solid rock.

Pulowech knew what it was. Booöins have power to enter stone; and one of them was trying to hide in the rock.

Pulowech cut off the knee with his hatchet. The cliff closed over the booöin, hiding him forever.

A little way on, Pulowech saw a foot sticking out of the rock. It he also cut off.

He had now slain two.

As he came out from the cliff, a little squirrel dragged herself, half dead from cold, into his path. Pulowech took her up and put her in his bosom.

"Rest, little one!" he said. "You shall fight for me to-day!"

He came to a lake. A flock of geese were swimming about, thrusting their long necks under the water.

Pulowech looked at them. "You are not what you seem!" he thought. They were booöins who had changed themselves into geese.

Pulowech hid; and when the geese swam near shore, he shot them with his arrows. He gathered them in, tied their heads together, and flung them over his shoulder.

The waters of the lake flowed into a river; and where the river began, Pulowech found a wigwam standing alone.

He dropped his geese by the door and entered. An old man was within. Pulowech no sooner saw him than he knew him for a boöoin.

The old man spoke to him sourly. He cooked meat and put it in a bowl as if to give it to him; but when Pulowech reached to take it, the old man snatched the bowl away.

"No," he said rudely, "I had rather my dog ate it!" He did this more than once.

Pulowech answered nothing.

"Did you see any strange thing to-day?" sneered the old man. He knew who Pulowech was.

"Nothing very strange," Pulowech answered; "I saw a knee and a foot sticking out of a cliff; I chopped them off. I shot some geese on a lake; they lie by your door, dead!"

This put the booöin in a fury. "Had you a dog," he screamed, "he should fight mine; we should see which of us is stronger!"

"I have a dog!" said Pulowech, smiling.

He took the squirrel from his bosom and put her down by the fire. She stretched herself, and sat up.

The booöin laughed.

"Dog, dog!" he called; and into the wigwam bounded a weisum,[1] an ugly beast big as a bear.

"Take her!" screamed the booöin, pointing.

Before the weisum could seize her, the squirrel leaped away, her tail a-quiver. In a trice she had grown as big as the weisum. She flew at his throat.

Over they rolled into the fire, scattering ashes and coals. Smoke and the smell of burning fur filled the wigwam. Pulowech

---

[1] Weī´- sŭm   See Note 31.

and the booöin ran about, the booöin shouting. The noise was deafening.

The squirrel began to weary. Pulowech stooped and patted her back; and there came leaping in two other squirrels, her sons. They grew to great size and sprang at the weisum.

"Call them off!" screamed the booöin. "The weisum is my grandmother's dog! She loves him."

Pulowech would not do this. The weisum was soon dead.

The old booöin wept aloud. "Alack, my grandmother!" he cried. "Her dear weisum is dead!"

He now spoke kindly to Pulowech.

"Grandson," he said, "let us take my canoe and go upon the river!"

"I will go," said Pulowech.

They were soon seated in the canoe. The current bore them toward a cliff, where the river entered a cave; on either side, the waves thundered against the rock.

Pulowech steered; but as he neared the cliff, he looked around. The booöin had just leaped ashore!

Pulowech did not try to turn the canoe. He steadied her with his paddle, bowed his head, and shot like an arrow into the cave.

He could not see to steer. The waters roared, and the canoe spun around and around in the dark. But Pulowech felt no fear. Calmly he sat in the bow, singing.[1]

After a while he saw a light ahead. He soon came out into daylight. He looked about him. There was a rocky cave in the bank of the river and smoke arose from its mouth.

"The booöin is there!" Pulowech thought.

He hid his canoe, and climbed to the cave. He heard voices within.

"I bring sad news, grandmother," said one. "The best of our band are slain. Your weisum is dead also!" It was the booöin that spoke.

"Who slays our band?" cried his grandmother, angrily.

"Pulowech, the partridge," answered the other.

His grandmother was in a rage. "Would Pulowech were here!" she cried; "I would roast him alive!"

She belonged to the porcupine folk, who love heat.

"Pulowech is dead," said her grandson. "I sent him afloat in the cavern!"

"But I am alive," said Pulowech; and he stepped into the cave. "Now roast me!" he said; and he sat down.

There was a great store of hemlock bark in the cave. The

[1] See Note 32.

booöin and his grandmother heaped the bark on the fire.

Hot flames roared upward, and the walls of the cave grew red with the heat. Pulowech sat unmoved.

The fire burned low at last.

Pulowech went out and fetched in more bark, until the cave was full. Then he closed the door.

"Do not slay us, grandson!" cried the booöin.

Pulowech answered, "You stole my wife!" He set fire to the bark and sat down.

Again flames roared upward. Red hot stones fell from the roof, and the sides of the cave cracked with the heat.

The fire died at last. Pulowech sat unhurt; but of the porcupines, nothing was left.

Pulowech arose and went to his canoe. He pushed off and sailed away, singing.

AND SAILED AWAY, SINGING

TWELFTH TALE

GLOOSKAP AND THE GIANT SORCERERS

A GIANT had three sons and a daughter; and all were sorcerers. Glooskap was their friend. The old giant even called him son, and often feasted him in his wigwam.

But at heart the old giant was evil; and his sons grew up worse than their father. They became booöins and hunted men. The land groaned for their wickedness.

All this came to Glooskap's ears, for it made a noise among the people. It grieved Glooskap.

"I will go and find if it is true," he said; and he departed.

The giants' wigwam stood near the sea; and as he went thither,

Glooskap thought how he should meet the booöins.

"I will not let them know me," he said to himself.

The old giant had but one eye. Glooskap made himself like him, even to his single eye. He entered the giant's wigwam, and found him sitting. Glooskap sat down and they began to talk.

By and by, the giant's sons came in. They saw Glooskap and the old giant by the fire talking, and looking just alike. They could not tell which was their father.

The giant's daughter had put a whale's tail in a pot and set it on the fire. The meat was now boiled. The girl put it into a bowl and gave it to Glooskap to eat.

He set it on his knees; but before he could take a mouthful, the eldest of the giant's sons snatched the meat out of the bowl.

"Beggar," he cried, "this is not for you!" He went out, taking the meat with him.

Glooskap did not show his anger. "The meat is mine," he said. "Your sister gave it to me!"

Sitting with the bowl on his knees, he thought, "I WISH THE MEAT BACK IN THE BOWL!" And the whale's tail, still hot, came flying in at the door and fell in the bowl. Glooskap began to eat.

When he had enough, Glooskap put down the bowl. He said nothing.

The giants looked at him, wondering. "He is a magician!" they thought.

The eldest of the young giants fetched in a whale's jaw, thick as a man's thigh. He took the ends in his hands and, with all his strength, bent the bone a little. He laughed, and gave the jaw to Glooskap.

"Let us see," he said, "what our little brother can do!"

Glooskap did not rise from where he sat. With thumb and finger of one hand, he snapped the whale's jaw as if it were a duck's wishbone!

The boöins were filled with awe. "He is indeed a magician!" they thought.

They brought out a great stone pipe, and filled it with strongest tobacco, that only sorcerers can smoke. They handed the pipe around.[1]

All smoked in turn, blowing out great clouds; the eldest handed the pipe to Glooskap.

"Let our brother try!" he said.

Glooskap filled the bowl anew. At one pull, he burnt all the tobacco to ashes, and blew the smoke from his nostrils in one great puff.

The giants were troubled. "He is a great magician!" they

[1] See Note 33.

216

thought.

Again Glooskap filled the pipe, and lighted it. One of the giants arose and made fast the door. He hoped Glooskap would strangle with the smoke.

But Glooskap puffed away, caring not a bit.

Not so the giants, who sat choking and coughing. At last, nearly strangled, they opened the door and ran out.

Glooskap followed them, smiling.

When all had gotten breath, the giants went apart and talked among themselves. They came to Glooskap.

"Our brother," they said, "is strong; but let us see his skill at ball!" They led him to a sandy plain in the bend of a river, not far away.

One of the giants put down a ball and the game began.

The ball was a live skull. It went rolling at Glooskap's heels, trying

to bite off his foot.

Glooskap laughed. "You play a merry game!" he cried, "but I too will have a ball!" He broke a bough from a tree and cast it on the ground.

The bough turned into a skull ten times bigger than the other. It rolled after the giants, bumping along and snapping its great jaws, until they cried for mercy.

Glooskap stamped upon the sand. With a mighty roar, waters came down from the mountains. The river rose, foaming, and overflowed the plain.

The giants fled; but the flood caught them. Struggling, they heard Glooskap singing above the waves.

As they heard, they became fish. The current swept them to the sea.

THEY BECAME FISH

F.N.WILSON

THIRTEENTH TALE

GLOOSKAP AND TUMILKOONTAWOO [1]

AGAIN Glooskap brought his family down by the sea. He found good fishing, and in the fall flocks of sea ducks came flying down from the north. He made him arrows and shot both ducks and geese. In the mornings, he fished or speared for eels.

But the weather grew windy. Heavy gales blew up, and the waves tossed his canoe so that Glooskap could do little fishing; nor could he spear eels in so rough a sea.

Weeks went by, but the weather stayed foul. The gales howled over the sea; and waves, mountain high, rolled inshore. Glooskap

[1] Tŭm - ĭl - kōōn´- tạ - wōō

219

no longer tried to put out in his canoe. He could not fish in such weather.

For days he sat in his wigwam, waiting for the wind to die. Still the gales blew.

There was little meat left in the wigwam. Glooskap's family were growing hungry.

"You must get us meat, grandson, or we starve," said the old Bear Woman.

Glooskap arose slowly. He went down to the shore to look for dead fish; for the waves sometimes cast fish against the beach, killing them. He walked along the beach, going north. The farther he went, the fiercer blew the wind.

"What makes the wind blow so?" he thought.

He came to a point of land that jutted out into the water. Just off the point rose a rocky islet. Something dark sat on the rock. Glooskap could not see what it was for the mist.

He bent his head to the wind and waded out. Fiercer rose the gale; Glooskap could hardly stand against it. He found shelter under the islet; and he stood and looked up.

On the top of the rock sat a giant eagle, flapping his great wings. As he moved them they fanned the wind which went rushing and raging over the sea.

"It is the Wind Bird," thought Glooskap.

The chill mist fell about him, and he shivered. A thought came to him.

"Grandfather," he called out, "are you not chilled in the wind?"

"No, grandson," answered the eagle.

"But grandfather," cried Glooskap, "your wings are wet with the mist. Let me carry you to the mainland. There is no mist there!"

The eagle sat awhile, flapping his wings.

"I will go, grandson," he said at last. "I am tired of sitting here on the rock."

"Good, grandfather!" cried Glooskap. He climbed the rock, bent his shoulders, and took the great eagle on his back. Glooskap climbed slowly down, and waded through the shallow water to the mainland; but as he came ashore, his foot slipped, and he stumbled. The eagle, falling from his shoulders, broke his wing.

"I am sorry, grandfather," cried Glooskap.

He lifted the eagle to his feet, and helped him get to a place out of the wind. He bound up the broken wing with willows, for splints.

"Does it hurt you, grandfather?" he asked.

"No, grandson," answered the eagle.

"Sit here, grandfather," said Glooskap. "Do not move your wing, or the bones will not knit. Each day I will bring you fish to eat."

Glooskap hastened home, and got out his canoe. There was no wind now, and the sea was like a pond. Glooskap could spear eels, or fish, as he liked. He brought in meat and fish daily, enough for his family and the eagle.

But with no breeze to stir the sea, the water grew stagnant. Fishes sickened and died; and a foul scum arose and overspread the sea.

Glooskap went to the eagle and unbound his wing.

"Grandfather," he said, "you may move your wing; but not hard, lest you hurt it!"

The eagle gently flapped his wings and a faint breeze swept over the water. It blew the scum from the surface of the sea.

Evening came, and the Bear Woman fetched Glooskap a bowl of steaming fish to eat. As he took it she said, "Grandson, did you not *plan* to fall and break the eagle's wing?"

Glooskap sat eating his fish. He said nothing, but his eyes were smiling.

The Bear Woman laughed. "We will call the eagle Tumil-koontawoo, or Broken Wing!" she said.

And now when a breeze blows off the sea, the Indians say, "Tumilkoontawoo fans his wings."

TUMILKOONTAWOO FANS HIS WINGS

FOURTEENTH TALE

GLOOSKAP AND ATOSIS[1]

ATOSIS the snake was evil. He had been a man; but he hated Glooskap and became a serpent that he might make war upon him.

Many times Atosis tried to slay him; but Glooskap was never one to be caught napping.

Glooskap's brother, the little marten, had a flute.[2] When he played upon it, the birds and beasts came up to hear its sweet music. Abistanooch called them his pets.

One day when Glooskap was gone, the little marten took his flute into the forest. On the way, he stumbled, and the flute fell from his hands. He picked it up, put it to his lips, and blew. It gave no sound.

[1] Át - ŏ - sĭs   [2] See Note 34.

224

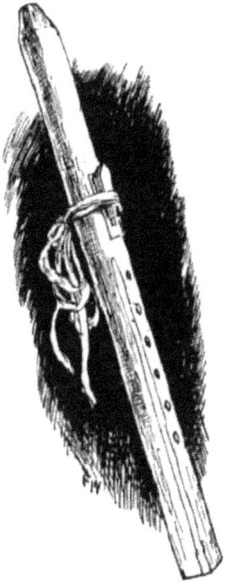

"My flute is broken!" cried the little marten. Again he blew. It was no use! The flute was silent. The little marten wandered on, weeping.

Evening came, and he lost his way. All that night he wandered, and the next, cold and hungry and weeping. It was the month for making maple sugar.[1] There was snow on the ground.

The third night out, the little marten came to a hollow in the forest. Below in the trees, he saw a light. He made his way down and came to a wigwam. A fire glowed within.

Timidly the marten entered. The firelight blinded him for a moment. When he could see, he was ready to die of fright.

A bark kettle full of boiling sap hung over the fire.[2] On the other side, watching the kettle, lay a great snake. It was Atosis, Glooskap's enemy.

"Kwai!" hissed the snake, "Welcome!" And he moved, rustling his scales.

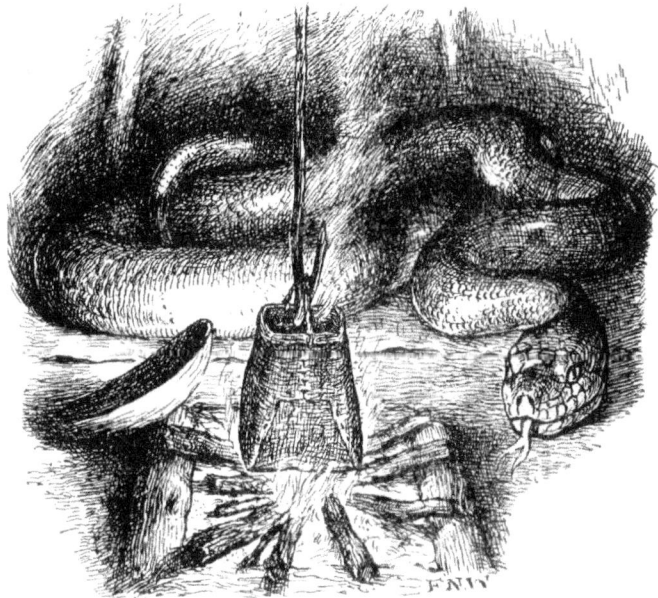

The little marten sat down by the door, in the place where wood

[1] See Note 35.   [2] See Note 36.

is piled. His heart went *pit-a-pat!* He was frightened.

"What do you want?" hissed the snake.

"To be warmed. I am cold and hungry!" said the little marten. Tears were in his eyes.

"I too am hungry!" hissed the snake. "I have not eaten for a month; and you are fat!"

And the snake moved again, spitting out his tongue.

The little marten shook with fright. "Do not kill me!" he begged; "I am Glooskap's brother."

The snake laughed aloud.

"I know you are Glooskap's brother," he hissed. "That is why I am going to eat you. I shall spit you on a stick, to roast over my fire!"

The little marten put his hands over his eyes and began to sob.

"Go, get the stick!" mocked the snake. "Get a straight one; it will not tear you!"

The little marten dared not say no. He arose and went out sobbing.

On the very evening the marten lost his way in the forest, Glooskap came back home. He found the old Bear Woman in the wigwam weeping.

"What has happened, grandmother?" he asked.

"Your brother, Abistanooch, has not come home," she answered. "I fear he is lost!" and she wept anew.

"Do not weep," cried Glooskap, "I will find him!"

Losing not a moment, he put parched corn in a pouch[1] to eat, caught up his hatchet, and hastened out. He came upon the little marten's tracks the next morning. The trail led into the forest. Swiftly, Glooskap followed.

The third night, he heard a voice in a hollow, singing. It was Abistanooch, calling his brother.

Glooskap hastened down, and soon saw the light from the snake's wigwam. Clearer rose the little marten's voice, singing against the snake kind. He was hunting a stick for a spit.

Glooskap heard, and knew all that had happened: how Atosis, for hate of him, had caused the flute to fall; how he had lured Abistanooch to his wigwam, and now sent him for a stick to spit him on.

Glooskap began to sing softly:

"Atosis bids you get a straight stick;
Get a crooked one, little brother!"

[1] See Note 37.

Abistanooch heard. Gladly he found a crooked stick and ran back to the snake's wigwam. Glooskap drew his hatchet and hid behind a fallen trunk.

Morn was breaking; a crow cawed overhead.

The snake raised his head as Abistanooch entered. "Did you get a straight stick?" he hissed.

"I got a crooked one," the little marten answered. "I will straighten it in the fire!"

He made a heap of coals in the fireplace and into it thrust one end of the stick.

The snake crept near to watch. He had never seen a stick straightened in the fire.

When the end that he held in his hand was steaming,

Abistanooch dragged the stick out of the fire. Atosis crept nearer, to see.

Suddenly, Abistanooch raised the stick and struck the snake over the eyes.

The great snake writhed and twisted with pain. Sparks had fallen into his eyes.

"Brother, brother!" cried the marten. He dashed out of the wigwam and ran straight for the trunk where Glooskap was hiding.

The snake followed, and raised his head to glide over the trunk.

Glooskap leaped up; and with a blow of his hatchet, slew him.

FIFTEENTH TALE

GLOOSKAP AND THE FROG CHIEF

UP in the mountains, there dwelt a village of Indians. Their town was only a dozen lodges, but the villagers thought it the finest in all the world.

A brook of clearest, cool water flowed by the town. Very proud were the Indians of their brook! They never tired drinking from it.

Indeed, it was all they had to drink. There was not a spring, not even a rain puddle, on the mountain side.

So the villagers drank for many years; but a summer came when their brook ran low. The maidens went each morning to the watering place,[1] to come back with kettles not half filled.

[1] See Note 38.

"The brook is failing!" they said.

"It will rise again," said the old women.

But the brook did not rise. Lower it sank, until the maidens came back one morning with empty kettles; the bed of the brook was dry.

The chief called the older men to a council. "What shall we do?" he asked. A pipe was passed. An old man arose. "We have heard," he said, "that farther up in the mountains is another village of Indians. It is they who stop our brook! Let a runner go and see if it is not so!"

He sat down, and the others cried, "Ho, ho!" The speech pleased them.

The chief called a fleet runner and said to him: "Go to the strange villagers. Ask them why they stop our brook!"

The runner set off, and the third day came to the strange village. There he saw what kept back the water. A dam was raised across the bed of the brook, backing the water into a wide pond.

Two men came out of a wigwam. They spoke to the runner, but did not ask him into their lodge.

"Why have you built the dam?" the runner asked them.

"Our chief did it; ask him!" the men answered. They told the runner that their chief lived in the pond.

The runner found the chief lying in the mud, sunning himself. He was big, fat, ugly. He had a wide mouth, and his yellow eyes stuck out like warts. His body was green.

"Ump!" he croaked like a great frog. "What do you want?"

"I want water," said the runner. "You have dammed our brook, and our villagers have no water to drink!"

The chief laughed; and swelling out his throat, he bellowed:

"Do as you please!

What do I care,

If you want water?

Go somewhere else!

Go somewhere else!"

"We must have water," cried the runner. "Our people have

nothing to drink!"

The chief laughed again. Lazily he sprang to the middle of the dam and made a hole in it with the point of an arrow. A little water flowed out.

The chief sprang back to his place in the mud and bellowed:

"Up and begone,
Up and begone,
Up and begone!"

The runner went away, sorrowful.

When he got home, his story made much stir among the villagers. For a few days, there was a little water in the brook, but it soon dried up and they were thirsty again.

The chief called another council.

"Unless we get water," he said, "we shall die of thirst. Let us choose our bravest warrior and send him to the strange village. There let him break the dam, or slay the chief and die fighting!"

The speech pleased the villagers. Each wanted to be the one to go.

Glooskap knew all that was going on in the world. It pleased him, who loved brave men, to see the villagers bent on breaking the dam. "I will help them!" he said.

He rose and dressed for war. The villagers were arming one of their own men to go, when Glooskap strode into the council.

Very terrible he looked. He wore a bonnet of eagles' feathers, and carried a lance in his hand. His cheeks were painted red, and green rings were around his eyes. Clam shells hung from his ears. Two eagle wings flapped from the back of his neck.

The Indians looked at him with awe. The young women thought him very handsome.

"What is this you do?" Glooskap asked them. The villagers told him of their plan.

"Let me go," Glooskap cried; "I will break the dam!"

He set off up the bed of the brook, and reached the strange village the third day.

At the edge of the town, he sat down on a log, to rest. No one came out to greet him.

A boy came by. Glooskap called to him, "Fetch me water to drink!"

"I cannot," answered the boy. "Our chief keeps all the water for himself."

"Go to your chief and get me water!" cried Glooskap.

He drew out his pipe and smoked, waiting. An hour had passed, when the boy came back with a cup of slimy, muddy water.

Glooskap threw the cup on the ground. "Take me to your chief!" he cried.

The boy led him to the dam. There in the mud lay the chief, sunning himself. Only his head was out of water.

He stared at Glooskap with his yellow eyes. "What do you want?" he croaked.

"I want a drink of good water!" Glooskap cried, angrily.

The chief laughed aloud, and bellowed:

"Ump, ump away with you,

Ump, ump, away with you!"

Glooskap rose in anger; and shouting his warwhoop,[1] ran the chief through with his lance.

And lo, the village disappeared;[2] and from the chief's body gushed a mighty river that burst the dam and went roaring down the brook's bed. The chief had swallowed all the waters of the brook.

Glooskap rose until he touched the clouds. He reached down, caught the chief, and squeezed him in his mighty grip. When he opened his fingers again, he held only a great, ugly bull frog! Glooskap tossed him into the stream.

[1] See Note 39.   [2] See Note 40.

A GREAT, UGLY BULL-FROG

SIXTEENTH TALE

GLOOSKAP'S RETURN TO THE VILLAGE

GLOOSKAP set off to return. His way led him down the bed of the brook. The cool waves went plashing by him. Glooskap was happy.

The third day, he reached the village of his friends. But no one came out to welcome him; and Glooskap was astonished to see no smoke rising from the wigwams. The village stood silent, empty; for a strange thing had happened.

All the Indians had gone down to the banks of the brook, to wait for the water to come. As they sat, dry and thirsty, they talked as hungry children do when they want something to eat.

"What would you want to do," one asked, "if our brook had water once more?"

"Live in the cool bottom," cried one, "and crawl about in the soft mud!"

"Dive all day long, from rocks and logs!" said another. He was a young man, and long-legged.

"Live among the stones at the edge of the brook, half on land, half in water!" cried a third.

"I," said a fourth, "would live in the water always, and never leave it!"

It chanced that they spoke in the hour that makes all wishes come true. So each had his wish.

The first became leech. The second became a spotted frog with long legs. The third became a crawfish; the fourth, a fish.

When the water from the dam came roaring down, all plunged in and swam away.

F.N.Wilson

SEVENTEENTH TALE

THE MEN WHO DISOBEYED GLOOSKAP

So the years rolled on, but the world was now growing wicked.[1] Men forgot the good that Glooskap had taught them. More and more they wanted to do their own will.

Glooskap was grieved, for he liked not wickedness. He took himself and his family to an island and dwelt there. It was even said he was minded to quit the world.

He did quit the world after a time; but before he went, he sent his messengers, the loons, throughout the land. "Any man who finds Glooskap may ask of him one wish!" they told the people.

[1] See Note 41.

Many set out; and to all that found him, Glooskap said, "You shall have your wish!"

But Glooskap took it ill that any should not do as he bade them. Some disobeyed; and these found that his gifts brought them no good luck.

Three men set out to find Glooskap. They went seven years and had nigh lost heart, when they heard dogs barking.

"Glooskap is there! We shall soon find him," the men said. But it was three months before they saw Glooskap's island. They passed over in a canoe.

Glooskap welcomed them. He feasted them many days, and they were getting ready to return home, when he asked them, "What do you want!"

The eldest was a simple, honest man. "I want to be a good hunter," he said. "Men think meanly of me, because I kill so few deer!"

Glooskap smiled. He liked men who thought not too much of themselves.

He gave the man a magic flute of wood. "Blow on this flute," he told him. "Deer and moose will come to you to be shot!"

The man thanked him and went away. He wondered to find himself, at the end of seven days, home in his village. He had been seven years on his way to Glooskap.

The second man was foolish. "I wish," he said, "to dance with the maidens whenever I will!'

Glooskap looked at him queerly. "A man should ask better than to be ever dancing!" he said.

"I care not!" the man answered. Glooskap fetched out a bag with its mouth tied, and gave it to him. "Take this," he said. "Open it when you get home; but do not look into it on the way!"

The third asked to be taught a strange, weird sound that makes all who hear it laugh and feel merry. In olden days, this sound was heard at every merrymaking. Now, only a few aged men can make it.

Glooskap bade Abistanooch fetch him a root. This he gave the man. "When you come in your wigwam," he said, "eat this root. Beware you do not eat it before!"

The two men scarce stopped to thank Glooskap. They set off, going different ways.

He with the bag was hardly out of sight, when he burned to know what was in it.[1] "It can do no harm to look!" he thought.

He untied the string, and *whut!* — out flew a winsome maiden! Her feet touched the ground, and she began to dance.

The man could not believe his eyes. He winked hard. "I must be asleep!" he thought. But *whut!* — out flew another maiden, and another, and another! In flocks they came, crying wildly.

The man longed to join in the dance. He held out his hands to the maidens, slipped, fell! Over him they danced, back, and over him again. "Help!" he cried, "help!" They gave no heed.

Hunters found him lying where he fell. No one knew what became of the maidens.

He of the weird sound fared no better. He was but a day's journey from his village, when he sat on a log to rest. He thought of the root, took it out, smelled it. The man longed to eat it.

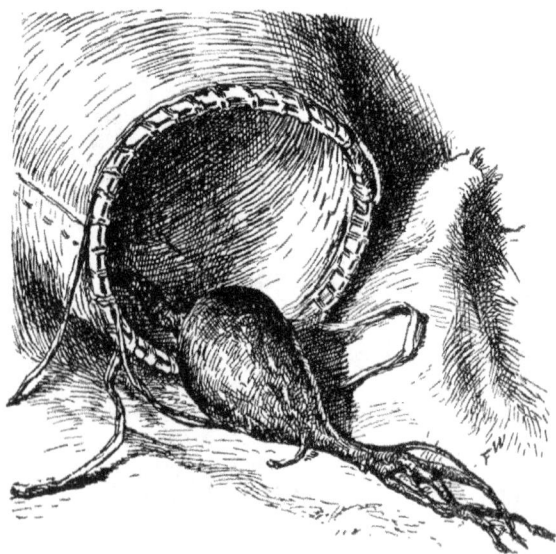

"Glooskap cannot know!" he thought, and he ate the root.

At once he could make the sound. He laughed as it came from his lips; and he went gayly on.

He was nearly home when a deer stepped into his path. The man was raising his bow to

[1] See Note 42.

shoot when the sound burst from him, — he could not stop it! The deer heard and leaped away.

"What ails me?" the man cried. Even as he spoke, the sound burst from him again.

It was so when he came to his village.

At first, all laughed at the sound; but the man could do nothing that it did not burst from him. He made it when he ate, when he slept! The villagers shunned him at last, weary with laughing.

With bitter heart, he wandered into the forest. "I care not if I die!" he cried.

Evening fell; darkness was coming on.

With a cry weird as the sound,[1] Pamola[2] the night-hawk swooped from the sky and bore the man off into the night!

[1] See Note 43.   [2] Pắ - mō - lạ

PAMOLA THE NIGHT HAWK

EIGHTEENTH TALE

KEEKWAJOO[1] AND KAKTOOGWASEES[2]

I. KEEKWAJOO IS MADE A MEGASOOWESOO[3]

KEEKWAJOO and Kaktoogwasees were young men who had each a wish. Keekwajoo was the elder; he longed to be a megasoowesoo, or enchanter. Kaktoogwasees wanted the daughter of a certain chief for his wife. This chief was a magician.

Neither of the men knew how to get the thing he longed for.

"Let us seek Glooskap!" said Keekwajoo. They journeyed long and came to Glooskap's wigwam on an island.

They entered as Indians do without knocking,[4] and found the Bear Woman and Abistanooch within. The old grandmother was

---

[1] Kéek - wa̧ - joo   [2] Kăk - tŏog - wa̧ - sēes   [3] mĕ - ga̧ - sóo - wĕ - soo   [4] See Note 44.

scouring a pot with rushes.[1] The marten was cleaning his pipe. He had his robe drawn about his knees as he sat.[2]

The Bear Woman spoke kindly to the strangers. "Sit here," she said; and she made a place for them behind the fire.

Glooskap came in later. "*Kwai!*—welcome!" he cried when he saw the strangers.

Then to his grand-mother: "These men have come far. Put on the pot and give them to eat!"

The Bear Woman stirred the fire and dropped a bit of meat, hardly a mouthful, into the pot. When it boiled, she took the meat into a wooden dish and handed it to Keekwajoo.

"Eat!" she said.

"We are mocked!" thought Keekwajoo, smiling; but he took the dish. He cut a piece off the meat and ate it. When he looked again in the dish, he was astonished to see the meat had grown to its first size.

"Wonderful!" he thought.

He and Kaktoogwasees fell to, and ate heartily. When they were done, there was meat in the dish as at the first.

Evening came. Glooskap asked the men what they wanted.

[1] See Note 45.   [2] See Note 46.

"To be a megasoowesoo," Keekwajoo answered. Kaktoogwasees said, "A chief has a daughter that I want for my wife. But the chief puts such tasks to those that seek her, that they die every one!"

Glooskap answered nothing. When the men had eaten again, and smoked, he gave them robes to sleep upon.

The next morning before sunrise, Glooskap called Keekwajoo, and led him to a river. "Bathe!" he said.

Keekwajoo plunged in and swam about. He came out with skin dripping.

Glooskap lent him a porcupine tail for a hairbrush;[1] and gave him a coat, leggings, and a magic hairstring.[2]

"The hairstring will give you the power you want," he told him.

Glooskap also gave him a wooden flute. "When you blow on it," he said, "you can charm all things!"

He bade him sing. Keek-wajoo did so and found his voice was low and sweet. He could not sing before.

Glooskap led him back to

the wigwam. "You are now a megasoowesoo," he said, "Your friend wants a wife. Go and help him win her!"

"I will go," said Keekwajoo, "if you will lend us your canoe!"

Glooskap laughed. "Take the canoe," he said, "but bring it back to me. Many borrow and forget to return it!"

"We will bring it back," said the two men.

Glooskap led them to the beach. A little way out in the water was a small, rocky island, covered with pines. "Behold my canoe!" said Glooskap, smiling.

The young men looked at the island. They did not know what to think.

"Wade out and climb into it!" said Glooskap.

They did so, and found themselves in a stone canoe. Pine paddles lay on the floor. The men chose each a paddle and sat down, Keekwajoo in the bow, Kaktoogwasees in the stern.

"Go!" called Glooskap.

The men dipped their paddles, and their canoe glided away towards the sea.

Weeks went by before the men reached the island where dwelt the chief. They landed, and Keekwajoo hid the canoe under a bush. They soon found the chief's village.

A man led them to the chief's lodge, a tall wigwam in the center of the town. They entered and stood.

The chief spoke kindly to them. "Sit here!" he said, and he spread a mat for them.

In the evening he made them a feast.[1] Afterwards, when they were alone, he asked, "What seek you?"

Keekwajoo answered for his friend. "Kaktoogwasees tires of dwelling alone! He seeks a wife."

The chief sat thinking.

"My daughter is fair," he said at last. "Let your friend fetch me the chepichkam's[2] head[3] for a gift!" This chepichkam was a great, horned serpent.

"May I help?" Keekwajoo asked.

"Yes," said the chief; for he thought, "The chepichkam will slay

---

[1] See Note 49.   [2] chē-pích-kam   [3] See Note 50.

them both!"

The men thanked the chief, and went to another wigwam to sleep.

At midnight, Keekwajoo arose and stole from the lodge. He made his way far into the forest until he came to a pit. It was the chepichkam's den. The moon had risen. The den looked black in the moonlight.

Keekwajoo rolled a log over the pit, drew his hatchet, and began to dance around the pit's mouth. Fast, faster, he danced.

After a while, an ugly head appeared and the chepichkam crept forth. It rested its head a moment on the log. Keekwajoo sprang forward, and with a blow, cut off the serpent's head.

He lifted the head by its horns and bore it to the wigwam. In the morning, Kaktoogwasees took it to the chief's lodge.

The chief was astonished. "I fear I shall lose my daughter," he thought.

But Kaktoogwasees was to have other tasks.

The chief invited him and Keekwajoo to a feast. After they had eaten, he led them to the door and pointed to a mountain. "Coast down yonder hill!" he said.

The top of the mountain was ragged, and white with ice. Its sides bristled with pines.

The chief's son brought out two toboggans,[1] as for a race; that for the strangers was to go first, and Keekwajoo was to steer.

Two strong men, booöins, got into the other toboggan. The chief hoped Kaktoogwasees would be spilled out on the snow, and the booöins, coming after him, would run him down.

The chief gave the word, and

the two toboggans shot down the mountain side. Halfway down, Keekwajoo's toboggan lurched, pitching Kaktoogwasees headlong. The two booöins laughed, "Ho, ho!" They did not know all this had been planned.

[1] See Note 51.

Keekwajoo turned his toboggan a little out of the path,[1] caught his friend, and pulled him aboard. This let the booöins' toboggan get ahead. Another instant, Keekwajoo was after them!

In the trees at the bottom of the mountain, the booöins' toboggan stopped. Keekwajoo's toboggan, flying over the booöins' heads, went on and struck the chief's wigwam, ripping it from end to end. It stopped in the fireplace.

The chief was angered, but could do nothing. "I fear I shall lose my daughter!" he thought.

Spring came, and the young men were running races. The chief called Kaktoogwasees to him.

"There is a young man," he told him, "a swift runner, who has never been beaten in a race. Go and run with him!"

Kaktoogwasees went to his friend. "What shall I do?" he asked. "I cannot run!"

"Take this flute," said Keekwajoo. "It will make you run!" He gave him Glooskap's flute. Keekwajoo put it in his medicine bag.[2]

The chief set an hour for the start. All the villagers came to look on.

The runners took their stand. They wore light moccasins on their feet. Their thighs and shoulders were bare.

"What is your name?" Kaktoogwasees asked.

"Men call me Weyadesk,[3] or Northern Light, because I am swift!" the other answered.

[1] See Note 52. [2] See Note 53. [3] We̱´-yạ-dĕsk

251

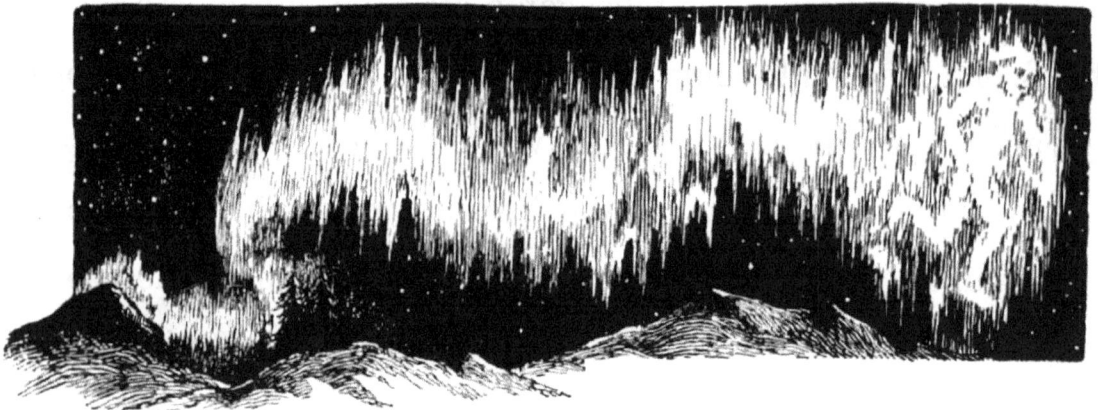

"I," laughed Kaktoogwasees, "am so fleet, men call me Wosogwodesk,[1] or Streak o' Lightning!"

The sun was just above the tree tops when the chief gave the word to go. The two runners darted off. They were out of sight in a twinkling.

Before noon, Kaktoogwasees returned. He had gone clear around the world, but was not tired. "I told you I was swift, like lightning!" he laughed.

He that was called Northern Light came in at evening. He was tired and out of breath, and his body trembled and quivered.[2] He had gone half round the world, and turned back.

The chief was angered and troubled. "I fear," he thought, "I shall lose my daughter!"

Kaktoogwasees was given one more task.

"A young man in my village has never been beaten at swimming," the chief told him. "Go and

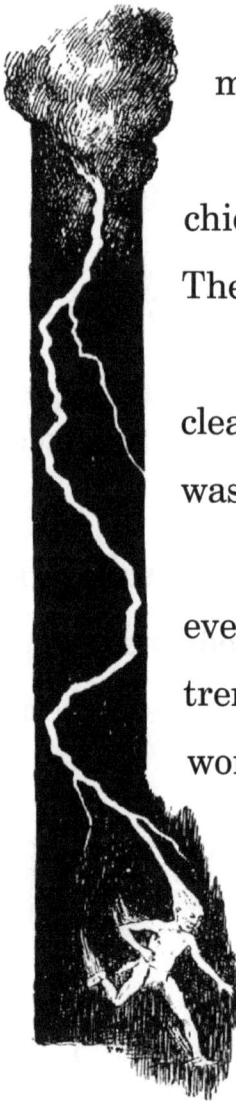

[1] Wō - sŏ́g - wō - dĕsk   [2] See Note 54.

252

dive with him."

"I will dive!" said Kaktoogwasees. He still had Glooskap's flute.

A day was set. The chief and all his villagers came down to the sea shore. The two divers stood on the edge of a rock, over the water.

"What is your name?" asked Kaktoogwasees.

"I am called Ukchi-gumoech,[1] or Sea Duck, for I dive far!" the other said, boasting. "Who are you?"

"Men call me Kwemoo, or Loon[2]!" laughed Kaktoogwasees.

At a word, the two men dived headlong. Breathless, the villagers waited.

The Sea Duck, after a time, came up for breath. Kaktoogwasees was not to be seen.

An hour passed, and another. Kaktoogwasees did not appear.

"He is drowned!" thought the villagers. Many went back to their homes.

Another hour had passed, when Kaktoogwasees came up, smiling. "I told you I was like a loon!" he laughed.

---

[1] Ŭk - chĭ - gŭm - ō - ĕch   [2] See Note 55.

The chief now made an end of the tasks.

"You have won!" he cried; and he led Kaktoogwasees to his wigwam. Keekwajoo was already there.

"The wedding feast shall be to-night!" the chief told them.

A crier was sent though the village to invite the people. Soon all was bustle in the lodges. Everybody was getting out his best clothes.

In the chief's wigwam, the floor was swept and made smooth for dancing. Hemlock boughs, for the fire, were piled near the door. Pots, heaped with good things to eat, stood by the fireplace. The guests brought their own feast bowls.

Again the chief was to see what power Glooskap could give.

The guests had come in, and the fun began. The young men sang; the drummers drummed; the dancers flew about, crying joyfully.

One old man had a log, carved with notches; over these he rubbed a stick, making sweet music.

At midnight all sat down to feast. The chief's

wife filled each one's bowl, saying, "Eat all of it!"

"I cannot eat so much!" cried a young man. His bowl was heaped with steaming fats.

The old men laughed. "I will help you eat it," said one, "but you must pay me your knife!"

Keekwajoo, meanwhile, sat by the door, looking on.

"Lazy Keekwajoo," laughed the others, "why do you not dance?"

Keekwajoo arose. Slowly at first, he began to dance around the fire. Fast, faster, he flew, now with his face forward, now with his back. Wondering, the others watched him. They saw that his feet were sinking into the hard floor.

Around he flew, sinking deeper at every turn. At last, only his head was seen above the ground.[1]

This ended the merrymaking. With a deep trench around the fireplace there could be no more dancing. All went home for the night.

[1] See Note 56.

III. The Return to Glooskap

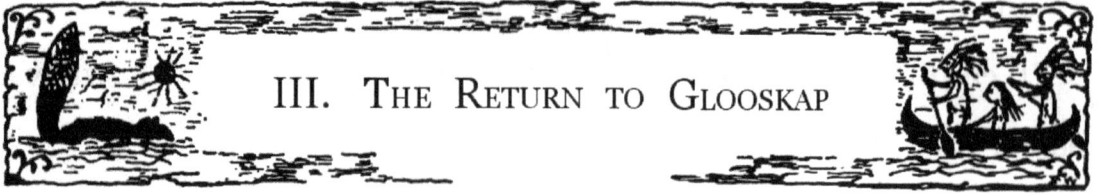

The next day Keekwajoo and the newly wed pair entered their canoe and sailed homeward. Kaktoogwasees paddled. His heart was light.

But their trials were not over.

They had been gone but a few hours when black clouds arose on the sea. A storm blew up. The canoe pitched upon the waves.

Keekwajoo laughed. "Your father's friends hope to wreck us!" he told the bride. "I will blow back the storm."

He knelt, facing the tempest, and filled his lungs. Puffing out his cheeks, he blew, wind against wind. Soon the clouds rolled back. The sun came out, and the sea was smooth again.

The men paddled gayly on. The wind sang in their ears, so fast they flew.

They had to pass one more danger.

At evening, as they were paddling along, a dark mass arose in their path. "What is it?" Kaktoogwasees asked.

Keekwajoo shaded his eyes. "It is Quabeet, the great beaver!" he said. "He is Glooskap's enemy, and ours!"

Quabeet lay with his head under water, his tail aloft. He thought to sink the canoe with a blow.

Keekwajoo steered straight for him.

"I am the hunter of beavers!" he shouted; and with his hatchet, he cut off Quabeet's great tail.

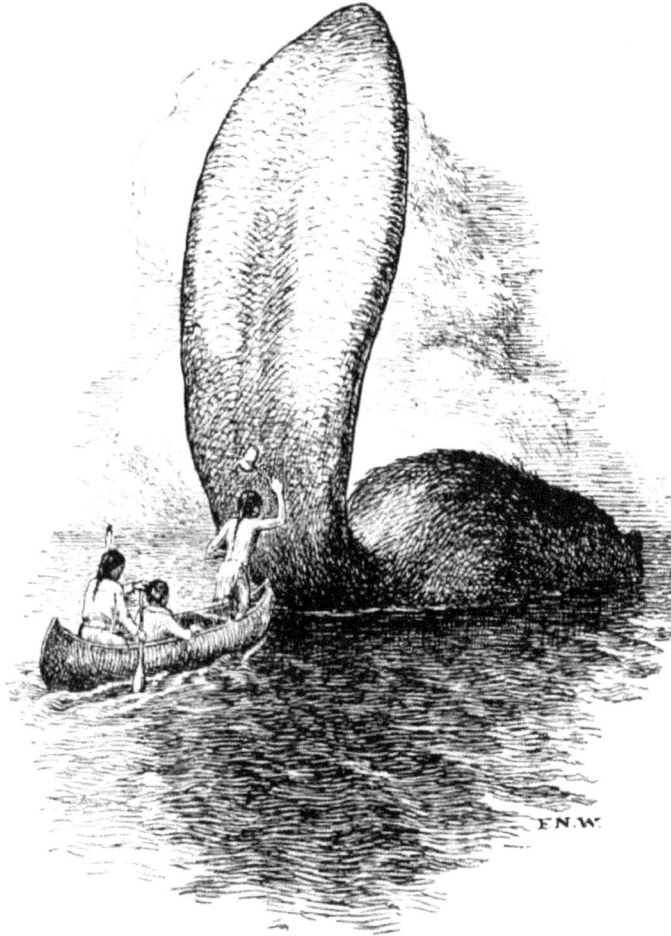

It fell into the water with a great plash, nigh overturning the canoe.

The sun was setting when Keekwajoo and his friends landed on Glooskap's island. Glooskap was waiting for them on the beach.

"I see you have brought back my canoe!" he said, smiling. He shoved it from the shore, and it became an island again.

Glooskap led the way to his wigwam.

"In all that you did, I helped," he said. "I saw you slay the chepichkam. I kept the toboggan from overturning!"

At the door, he paused.

"Go," he said to Keekwajoo, "dwell with magicians. You," he said to Kaktoogwasees, "live with your bride. If you have need, think of me and I will come!" Then he entered his wigwam.

"GO" HE SAID & ENTERED HIS WIGWAM

NINETEENTH TALE

THE GOING OF GLOOSKAP

BUT the time came when Glooskap had to quit the world. Men were growing more evil; and they no longer obeyed or loved him. "Glooskap," they cried, "who is he?" And they mocked at him.

Such is the world's way.

Men and beasts spoke then one language; and the Abnakis even called the beasts and birds their brothers. This peace lasted while Glooskap was chief.

When they no longer loved Glooskap, men began to hate one another. Then came wars. Everywhere were fighting and strife.

Glooskap sorrowed greatly. "I will forsake the land," he said at last. "The people weary me with their quarrels."

He made ready to go.

On the shore of the sea he got ready a feast; and to it he invited the people. The birds and beasts came also, for in those days they were as men. Glooskap welcomed all.

They ate, and there was much dancing and drumming. At last Glooskap stood up to speak.

"I go," he said, "into the west. Some day I will return!"

His stone canoe lay on the beach. Glooskap dragged it to the water and stepped in. He pushed off, singing.

From the shore, the people watched the canoe rising, falling, on the waves. Smaller it grew, until it was a dot on the water. The song became fainter, ceased. Silence fell on all.

In the west the sun had set. Twilight was falling.

Sadly the people turned to go, when a strange thing came to pass.

Men and beasts, who had spoken one language, found they could no longer understand one another. The people fled in fear to their wigwams. The beasts slunk to their dens. Never again were they to meet in council.

All knew, too late, that their friend had departed.

The snowy owl flew into the forest calling, *"Koo, koo, skoos, — O, I am sorry!"*

The loons go wailing up and down the land; and at night the wolves, Glooskap's servants, howl mournfully for their master.

Men and beasts now slay each other and are never happy. There will be no peace until Glooskap comes.

THE GOING OF GLOOSKAP

TWENTIETH TALE

GLOOSKAP AND THE THREE SEEKERS

NOT all men had forgotten Glooskap. Some, like the owl, loved him and mourned his going. Among these it was told that they who had need might yet find him; but the way to him was long and full of danger.

Three men were unhappy. Each had an evil in his life and knew not how to get rid of it. "Let us seek Glooskap," said one, at last. "He will help us!"

They left home in the spring, when birds were singing. All summer they journeyed, over rivers, through forests. Fall came, and winter, and spring again; and they had not found Glooskap. They would not turn back.

At midsummer they came to a path, and following it came out by a river that widened into a lake. The path went on around the lake. It was marked in places by blazed trees.

"There is a wigwam ahead!" said the men. "The trees are barked on the side towards us."[1]

They hastened on and came to a point of land that went out into the lake. They climbed a hill and saw white smoke rising at the end of the point. They made their way thither and found a wigwam.

They entered. A warrior sat at the right of the fireplace, smoking a pipe. An old woman was stirring a pot on the fire. A mat was at the left of the door, as if some one sat there.

"*Kwai,* — welcome!" said the warrior. He made a place for the strangers to sit, and offered them his pipe. He did not ask who they were.

As the men sat resting, they heard the plash of a paddle and a sound as of a canoe dragged up on the beach. The door-skin opened and a youth entered. He was slim, and his clothes fitted him neatly.

[1] See Note 57.

"Grandmother," he called, "here is meat for you!"

The old woman tottered to the door and fetched in four beavers.

She brought her skinning knife and sat, to make the meat

ready for the pot. But her eyes were weak, and her hands shook; and the knife fell from her grasp.

The warrior spoke. "Younger brother, you cut up the meat!"

The youth did so; and the old woman dropped the pieces into a pot. When the pot had boiled, all supped.

The travelers rested many days in the wigwam. All this time the warrior asked them nothing.

Then a thing happened that showed them their hosts were not common folk.

The old woman had seemed to grow more aged every day. Her back became more and more bent; and her hands shook so that she could hardly stir the fire when it was low.

The travelers pitied her. "She will die," they thought.

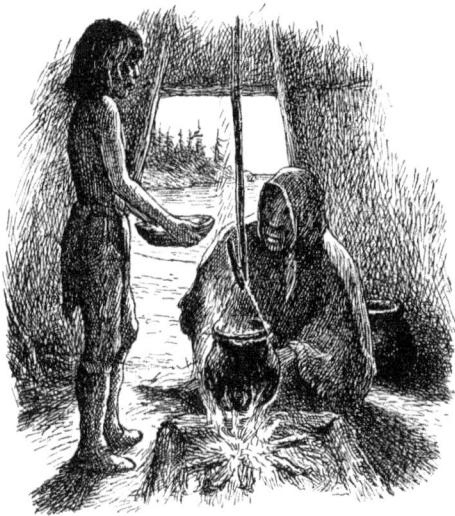

One morning, as she bent over the fire, the warrior said, "Younger brother, bathe your grandmother's face with water!"

The youth fetched a bowl, filled it, and gave it to her.

As the water touched the old woman's face, a change came over her. Her cheeks grew plump; her hair that had been white, became black and glossy, and her bent back grew straight.

From a bag, she brought out a garment of softest skins and put it on; and now she stood before them, a woman, young, sweet-faced, graceful. The travelers had never seen any one more lovely.

"The man is a magician," they thought; and it awed them.

The warrior now spoke to them. "Who are you, and what do you seek?"

"We are Abnaki men," they answered. "We seek Glooskap."

"I am he!" said the warrior. His face changed as he spoke, and he grew younger. The others saw that he was indeed Glooskap.

The first of the travelers told his wish.

"I am a wicked man," he said, "quick to anger; and I speak ill of others. I long to be good, that men may love me!"

"I am poor," said the second; "I kill not enough meat to give my children. I want to be rich, that I may care for them!"

"I," said the third, "am ugly, and my body is crooked. I long to be handsome, that all may welcome me when I come to their wigwams."

Glooskap sat and thought. "You shall have as you ask," he said at last.

He arose, and from his medicine bag brought three small boxes. He gave one to each of the travelers. "Do not open these," he said, "until you come to your village!"

He also gave them suits of clothing, of softest skin, white and beautiful. "Put these on," he said.

The travelers did so, casting away their own worn-out

garments. They were now ready to depart.

"Where is your way home?" Glooskap asked them.

"We do not know," they answered. "We were many months coming. We do not know our way back."

"I will guide you home," said Glooskap.

The next morning he put on his belt and led the men forth. Before noon, they came to the top of a mountain. Glooskap pointed to another mountain in the distance. "That," he said, "is near your home!"

At mid-afternoon, they came to the top of the other mountain. The men wondered to come to it so soon.

Glooskap stood and pointed with his finger. "There," he said, "is your village!"

The men looked, and saw they were in their own land.

Glooskap now left them. With happy hearts, the three Indians climbed down the mountain side. They reached home before sunset.

None knew them when they came to their wigwams, not even their kin. "Where did you get such rich clothes?" their friends asked them.

They told their story.

When they had ended, they opened their boxes. Within was a sweet-smelling ointment, which they rubbed over their flesh. A marvelous change then came over them.

He that was ugly and had a crooked back, became straight and handsome. He was welcomed in every wigwam.

He that was poor had his wish, and became rich. Moose and deer ran to him to be shot. Fish swarmed into his nets. He did not forget that he had been poor. He gave to all who had need.

He that was wicked became gentle and good. Of all, his blessing was greatest.

HIS BLESSING WAS GREATEST

TWENTY-FIRST TALE

GLOOSKAP AND THE THREE MEN WHO BECAME PINES

THE story of the three travelers and their gifts made much noise in the land. It was told in every village, at every camp fire. Old men, listening, nodded their heads and said, "We did so in our youth!" The young men burned to do as the travelers had done.

Three brothers, hearing the story, were minded to go to Glooskap. They were stout lads, but vain and knowing little of the big world. "We can do what others have done!" they boasted. And they set off.

They journeyed long and entered a land where no birds sang. They climbed a high mountain; to go down was even harder, for the mountain overhung a plain below. They reached the ground more dead than alive.

A little way on, they saw a thing to freeze their blood! Two great serpents lay with heads on either side of the road. The serpents hissed, darting out their tongues.

The brothers dared not go back. "We cannot climb the mountain!" they thought. Taking heart, they ran so swiftly between the serpents' heads, that the poisoned tongues did not touch them.

A worse thing was before them. It was a thick, heavy cloud, like a wall; and it rose and fell, rose and fell, crushing all beneath. No one knew when it would fall.

"We cannot go back!" thought the brothers again. As the cloud rose, they darted under. They came out just as it fell.

They now found themselves in Glooskap's land. They wondered to see it so fair.

They spied Glooskap's wigwam standing between two others. All were of bark. Glooskap's was the tallest.

Glooskap welcomed the men and gave them a beaver's tail to eat.[1] They asked him who lived in the other lodges.

"My two friends," he answered.

When they had done eating, Glooskap led the men out to see his friends.

In the first wigwam was Koolpujot,[2] a strange man. He has no bones and cannot move himself. Twice a year Glooskap rolls him over, in spring toward the east; in autumn, toward the west.

Koolpujot's breath sweeps down forests. His look brings frost, hail, rain, sunshine.

All this means the seasons.

In the other wigwam dwelt Kookwa,[3] or Earthquake. This mighty man can rush along underground. He makes the earth tremble and shake at his power.

The brothers rested a few days. Glooskap then asked them, "What do you want?"

The first was a tall man, vain of his looks. His hair was combed high and was thick with bear's grease; and a turkey feather waved in his scalp lock.

[1] See Note 58.   [2] Kōŏl - pŭ - jŏt   [3] Kōŏk - wạ

271

"I wish," he said, "to be the tallest Indian in the world."

The second was pleased with Glooskap's land. "I should like to live here always!" he said.

"I want to live to a great age," said the third, "and have good health!"

Glooskap looked at them gravely.

"You shall have as you wish," he said, "but not, I fear, to your liking!"

He arose and went to the door. "Kookwa," he called, "come!"

Earthquake came out of his lodge, yawning mightily. He had been asleep.

"Take these men," said Glooskap, "and set their feet in the ground!"

Kookwa led the brothers to the side of a knoll. One by one, he lifted them and stood them in a row, with their feet in the ground. They became three pine trees.

So each man had his wish.

He that would be tall, lifts his head above all the forest trees.

The turkey feather, now a tuft of green, waves in the wind. All day long, in the pine forests, the tree may be heard whispering:

"Oh, I am such a tall man;
Oh, I am such a big Indian!"

The second, who would dwell in Glooskap's land, is there still. With his roots in the ground, he cannot leave.

The third, who would live long, has his wish. If the winds have not blown him down, he stands as Kookwa left him!

THEY BECAME PINE TREES

TWENTY-SECOND TALE

THE LAST BATTLE

GLOOSKAP still lives. His wigwam stands on an island far in the west. It is a long wigwam, and its door opens toward the sunrise, where the Abnakis dwell.

There Glooskap sits on a mat, and makes arrows. He sings strange songs as he works.

No one comes to his door.   He will let none enter.

Already the wigwam is half full of arrows. When it is filled, Glooskap will come forth to make war. He has not forgotten the evil that men did him.

Many think he will slay all mankind. Others, very old men, say: "It is not so! He will slay the wicked. The good who die go to Glooskap's land. There live the Bear Woman and Abistanooch; and Glooskap's two dogs are with him, leaping and barking as of yore!"

GLOSSARY OF INDIAN NAMES

English equivalents are in Italics

Ă-bĭs-tắn-ōōch,	*Marten;* name of Glooskap's adopted brother.
Ăb-nạ́-ki,	*East Folk;* name given by other Algonkins to the tribes of New England and Nova Scotia.
Át-ō-sĭs,	*Snake.*
bōóch-kạ-jōō,	*A bark basket.*
bōō-ó-ĭn,	A cannibal sorcerer.
Bōót-ŭp,	*Whale.*
chē-pích-kạm,	A fabulous horned serpent.
Glōós-kăp,	*Deceiver;* the Abnaki creator and demi-god.
Kăk-tōóg-wạ-sēēs,	*Little Thunder;* name of an Indian.
Kēék-wạ-jōō,	*Badger;* name of an Indian.
Kít-pōōs-ă-gŭn-ō,	The name of a giant, Glooskap's friend.
kōō, kōō, skōōs,	*Oh, I am sorry;* an exclamation.
Kōók-wạ,	*Earthquake.*
kōók-wĕss,	A cannibal giant.
Kōól-pŭ-jŏt,	*He-who-is-rolled-over-with-hand-spikes;* personification of the revolving seasons.
kūss,	*stop;* an exclamation.
kwaī,	*welcome;* an exclamation.

Kwḗ-mōō,	*Loon.*
Mál-sŭm,	*Wolf;* the name of Glooskap's brother.
Mḗek-ō,	*Squirrel.*
mĕ-gạ-sóō-wĕ-sōō,	An enchanter whose magic lies in a wooden flute.
Mík-chĭch,	*Turtle;* the name of Glooskap's adopted uncle.
Mṓo-ĭn,	*Bear.*
Pắ-mō-lạ,	*Nighthawk.*
Pík-tōōk,	*Bubbling Air;* name of a place on the coast of Nova Scotia.
Pṓ-gŭmk,	*Fisher.* The fisher is an animal of the weasel kind.
Pók-ĭn-skwĕss,	The name of a sorcerer.
Púl-ō-wĕch,	*Partridge.*
Quä-bḗet,	*Beaver.*
Tḗe-ạm,	*Moose.*
tḗ-pēe,	*A lodge.*
Tŭm-ĭl-kṓon-tạ-wōō,	*Broken Wing;* name of the wind eagle.
Ŭk-chï-gŭm-ō-ĕch,	*Sea Duck;* name assumed by a diver.
ŭk sāy,	*Oh, horrible!* an exclamation.
weí-sŭm	A fabulous beast.
Wḗ-jĕk,	*Tree Partridge;* Pulowech's cousin.
Wḗ-yạ-dĕsk,	*Northern Light;* name assumed by a runner.
Wín-pĭ,	The name of a sorcerer.
Wō-sóg-wō-dĕsk,	*Lightning Flash;* name assumed by Keekwajoo.

EXPLANATORY NOTES

1, *page 131;* "An eagle's feather stood in his scalp lock." The tail feathers of the golden eagle were worn almost universally over North America. These feathers in eagles under two years of age are of a pure white, with dark brown or black tips, and are much prized. As the eagle grows older, the white parts of the plumes become a mottled brown, and are less valued.

A warrior earned his right to wear eagles' plumes. Their significance varied with the tribe. Among the Minitaris, an eagle feather in the hair meant, "I have been in battle and struck an enemy."

Eagle hunting was a highly honored occupation.

2, *page 137;* "to bury fish in their fields that the corn might grow." The custom of burying a fish in each hill of maize, to fertilize it, was taught our early Pilgrim fathers by the New England Indians.

3, *page 137;* "He called her his grandmother." That is, his grandmother by adoption. Grandmother and grandfather are terms of respect.

4, *page 138;* "Glooskap called him his younger brother." His adopted younger brother. The terms *elder* and *younger* also indicate rank. The elder has precedence. Indian etiquette is well defined.

5, *page 142;* "and he made a fire by his brother's grave." An Algonkin custom to light the ghost on its four days' journey to the spirit land.

6, *page 143;* "He covered it with bark sewed in wide strips." There were several of these strips stretching around the wigwam, and overlapping like shingles. They were held in place by overlying poles, bound to the tent poles beneath. When camp was moved, only the bark strips were taken. On the prairies, where wood was scarce, the tent poles were often borne along with the moving camp.

7, *page 144;* "Glooskap had two wonderful dogs." Before white man came, the Indians had but one domestic animal, the dog. He was used in hunting, as a watch dog, and as a beast of burden. The parboiled flesh of a young dog is thought a delicacy by some tribes.

8, *page 145;* "A wooden platter lay in the bottom of the canoe." With a piece of flint for a knife, the Indians carved beautiful bowls or platters of wood. A large knot was split from the trunk of a tree, and the bowl painfully worked into shape. Such bowls were used for feast bowls and to toss dice in gaming.

9, *page 146;* "It may be he did so to gain power." That is, supernatural power, magic power. No Indian started off to war without first seeking *power* of the spirits.

10, *page 149;* "She is smoking Glooskap's pipe." A whale, coming up and blowing the vapor-laden air from its lungs, sends up a fine spray, not unlike smoke; hence this curious myth.

11, *page 150;* "She begged Glooskap to fetch her some firewood." This was woman's work. We may suspect that the witch sought to humble Glooskap.

12, *page 151;* "warmed Glooskap some broth." The light broth in which dried meat is boiled is used as a hot drink. It is merely beef tea.

13, *page 152;* "The old man was a *booöin.*" A booöin is a sorcerer or conjurer, especially an evil conjurer who eats human flesh; our word *powwow* is a slightly altered form of the word.

14, *page 154;* "marks scratched upon it told Glooskap all he needed to know." The eastern tribes were skillful at picture writing. Messages in pictographic signs are still exchanged by older Indians.

15, *page 155;* "but his clothes were good." The sleek coat of the marten, as of all members of the weasel family, will hardly reveal the starved condition of its owner.

16, *page 157;* "Glooskap came upon a town of many lodges." These, of course, were the loons' nests.

17, *page 160;* "Come and sit back of the fire." The place of honor in a wigwam is back of the fireplace.

18, *page 163;* "Glooskap laid a great belt of wampum beads on his arm." Wampum beads were cut out of shells. To cut one bead was a day's labor. Beads were of two colors, white and blue. They were used as a rude form of money.

19, *page 166;* "They will ask you to play a game of ball." Our game of lacrosse is derived from a form of the Indians' game of ball.

20, *page 167;* "you must hang in the smoke." This amusing part of the myth is perhaps suggested by the custom of smoking meat over the wigwam fire.

21, *page 169;* "while the women dried meat." Meat for the winter was sliced thin and dried on scaffolds in the open air, or over a slow fire. The dried meat was packed away in skin bags.

22, *page 170;* "and soon came upon a fat cow moose." The flesh of the cow is more esteemed, because more tender. The buffalo-hunting Indians, unless game was scarce, hunted only cows.

23, *page 173;* "All night they danced by the firelight." Indians will often dance and sing an entire night. Singing and dancing were marks of rejoicing, especially at the death of an enemy.

24, *page 181;* "Glooskap and the giant sat, smoking and telling tales." Telling tales was a common way of passing the evening, especially in late autumn and winter. Among some tribes it was forbidden to tell the tribal myths or to talk of the spirits in summer, when nature was *alive.*

25, *page 185;* "boochkajoo, bark basket." Baskets for carrying objects on the back were common in all the tribes. A thong from the basket passed over the carrier's forehead or shoulders.

26, *page 188;* "They met in a long lodge." Lodges, built long to hold a large company, are still found among the Chippewas. In shape they are not unlike an old-fashioned covered wagon, or prairie schooner.

27, *page 189;* "She . . . sat down between two witches, the Toad Woman and the Porcupine Woman." These witches were in human shape.

28, *page 196;* "strapped in a cradle, like a babe." An Indian babe was kept strapped in his cradle until about a year old. On the march, the cradle was borne on the mother's back, held by a thong across her forehead or shoulders. A wooden bow, bent around in front of the baby's face, protected him in case of a fall. To this bow, playthings were tied; or thongs, to protect the babe from mosquitoes.

We suspect Abistanooch was in his totemic, or animal shape.

29, *page 198;* "and wedge." Wedges for splitting wood were commonly used by the Indians. They were made of wood, of a piece of deer's antler, or of a buffalo horn.

For a buffalo horn wedge, the horn was dipped in marrow fat and held over a fire until soft; a piece of ash wood was then driven into the hollow horn, straightening it. With such rude tools, trees of considerable size were split, and even made into planks.

30, *page 200;* "Pulowech." Pulowech is Micmac for the partridge or ruffled grouse.

31, *page 210;* "weisum." A fabulous beast, owned by booöins and sorcerers. The struggle between Meeko and the weisum is a test of their masters' magic.

32, *page 212;* "Calmly he sat in the bow, singing." Singing a magic song to call the spirits to aid him.

33, *page 216;* "They handed the pipe around." Indians smoke by inhaling into the lungs and expelling through the nostrils. Each smoker inhales a few whiffs, and passes the pipe to the next in the circle. Only the tips of the lips are pressed to the stem of the pipe; it is never taken into the mouth.

34, *page 224;* "the little marten had a flute." The flute is a rude wooden instrument, pierced with holes, and blown from the end like a fife. Simple melodies may be played upon it.

35, *page 225;* "It was the month for making maple sugar." Maple sap runs the latter part of February and the first of March. Our art of making maple sugar was learned of the Abnaki Indians.

36, *page 225;* "A bark kettle full of boiling sap hung over the fire." Such kettles were made until recently by the Chippewas. A fire of wood was let burn until the blaze died down, when the kettle was swung close to the coals, but not touching them.

37, *page 227;* "he put parched corn in a pouch." Travelers often carried a lunch of parched corn. A ball of pounded parched corn or sunflower meal was carried as an emergency ration by Minitari warriors.

38, *page 230;* "to the watering place." An Indian village was always pitched near a stream or lake. A place was commonly set apart as a watering place where the village maidens came to fill their kettles, gossip, and visit. The young men, dressed in their gayest, often came down to help their sweethearts fill their kettles.

39, *page 236;* "and shouting his warwhoop." There is really no such thing as a warwhoop, as white people usually understand it. Indians when excited shout or yell, just as white men do. A German shouts *hoch*, and Englishman shouts *hurrah,* and Americans have their yell heard on many a football field. Indians have their yell also.

40, *page 236;* "And lo, the village disappeared." Leland thinks that Glooskap here represents the rays of the vernal sun piercing the spirit of the frozen river.

41, *page 239;* "the world was now growing wicked." The Indian had no clear conception of sin as the Christian has; but he had a horror of ingratitude.

42, *page 242;* "he burned to know what was in it." Indians have a high regard for self-control. No vice is more severely condemned than idle curiosity.

43, *page 243;* "With a cry weird as the sound." The night hawk has the habit of swooping to earth with a prolonged booming sound made by the vibrating quills of the wings.

44, *page 244;* "They entered as Indians do without knocking." But a polite cough may be given just outside the door, by an entering visitor. The Mandans and Minitaris hung hollow buffalo hoofs to the skin door of the lodge; these made a rattling noise when the door opened.

45, *page 245;* "The old grandmother was scouring a pot with rushes." Rushes were widely used for scouring and polishing. The author owns a bow polished and smoothed with these rushes, as with emery paper.

46, *page 245;* "He had his robe drawn about his knees as he sat." Indians had no chairs. Often the robe was drawn about the knees and around the hips, bracing the back as one sat.

47, *page 246;* "Glooskap lent him a porcupine tail for a hairbrush." The skin of a porcupine's tail was mounted on a stick with the ends of the quills clipped or burned off, and used as a hair brush. Such brushes are still in use.

48, *page 246;* "and a magic hairstring." These hairstrings were often profusely ornamented with wampum beads.

49, *page 248;* "In the evening he made them a feast." This was a proper thing to do when distinguished strangers came to the village. The Abnakis had the custom of requiring every guest to eat all the food given him; if unable to do this, the guest must hire some one present to help him empty his bowl.

50, *page 248;* "fetch me the chepichkam's head." The chepichkam was a fabulous horned serpent with supernatural powers.

51, *page 250;* "The chief's son brought out two toboggans." The Indian sledge, or toboggan, is made of two thin boards curving upward at the forward end, and bound side by side with thongs. It is drawn by hand or with dogs. The toboggan is especially useful on ground that is irregular and uneven; and it glides easily over soft snow where a sled with runners would sink and become clogged. Coasting on a toboggan was a favorite winter sport with the Indians.

52, *page 251;* "Keekwajoo turned his toboggan a little out of the path." He did this by dragging one foot in the snow on the side toward which he wished to turn.

53, *page 251;* "Keekwajoo put it in his medicine bag." The medicine bag was a pouch, often worn about the person, and containing the Indian's "medicine" or sacred object.

54, *page 252;* "and his body trembled and quivered." In this myth, the two runners personify lightning and the northern light. Indians believe the world to be a great island; to go around the world would mean to pass quite around the island's circumference. This the lightning easily does, as may be seen in any storm, when the lightning flashes about the whole circuit of the heavens. The aurora borealis, or northern light, is seen only in the northern half of the sky; and it has a curious quivering, trembling motion, quite unlike the bold, strong flash of lightning.

55, *page 253;* "Men call me Kwemoo, or Loon." The loon is a more powerful diver than the sea duck.

56, *page 255;* "only his head was seen above the ground." To dance a trench in the ground was the severest test of Abnaki magic.

57, *page 263;* "The trees are barked on the side towards us." When trees were blazed, it was on the side *from* the wigwam, that the blazed marks might be seen by one coming *toward* the wigwam.

58, *page 271;* "and gave them a beaver's tail to eat." Beaver's tail is a delicacy among the Indians.

SUPPLEMENT

SUPPLEMENT

HOW TO MAKE AN INDIAN CAMP

YOUNG folks who want to grow up strong and healthy should live, like the Indians, a great deal out of doors; and there is no pleasanter way to do this than in an Indian camp. Such a camp you should learn to make; it may be pitched in a field or wood, in a park, or in your back yard.

THE TENT

The Indians made many kinds of lodges. The commonest is a tent of poles, covered with skins or bark. In the West, a skin-covered tent is called a tepee.[1]

Of late years, tepees have been covered with canvas, for skins are now hard to get; but the pattern of the cover is unchanged.

A tepee, ten feet high, big enough for four boys, is easily made. Study the pattern designs on the next page.

Sew strips of eight-ounce duck into a rectangular sheet, twenty feet long by ten feet wide.

With scissors, cut out a semicircular piece, *BCD,* in Fig. 1; *AB, AC,* and *AD* should measure each ten feet.

Cut out triangular pieces *AKJ* and *ALM; JK, AK, AL,* and *LM* should measure each one foot.

Cut the slits *NO* and *HI,* each six inches in length.

The pieces *STUV* and *WXYZ* are for smoke flaps; *ST* should measure five feet; *UV,* four feet; *VS,* two feet; and *TU,* one foot. Like measurements apply to *WXYZ.*

At *S* and *X,* in the smoke flaps, sew small, three-cornered pieces for pockets.

Sew the smoke flaps to the cover so that *UV* is fitted to *NM,* and *ZY* to *HJ.* The pockets of the smoke flaps should lie on the weather side of the cover.

Cut out the segments *EFG* and *PQR* for the door; *GE* and *PR* should measure two and one half feet each; and *EB* and *DR,* one

---

[1] té-pēē

287

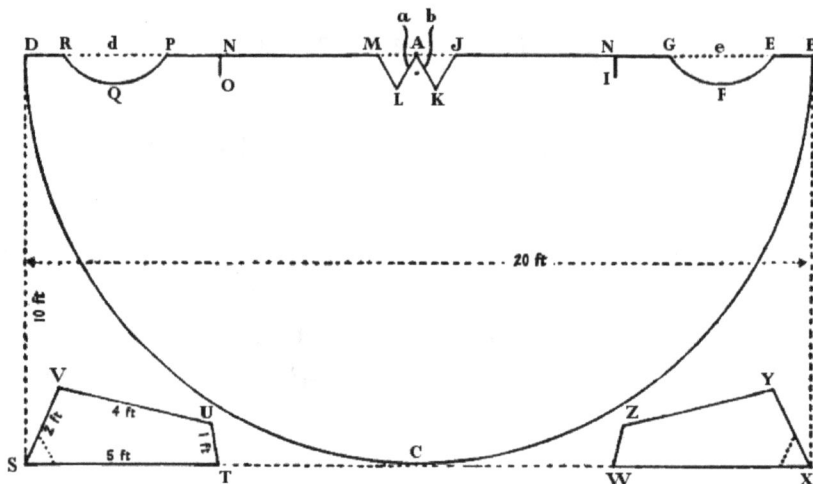

FIG. 1.

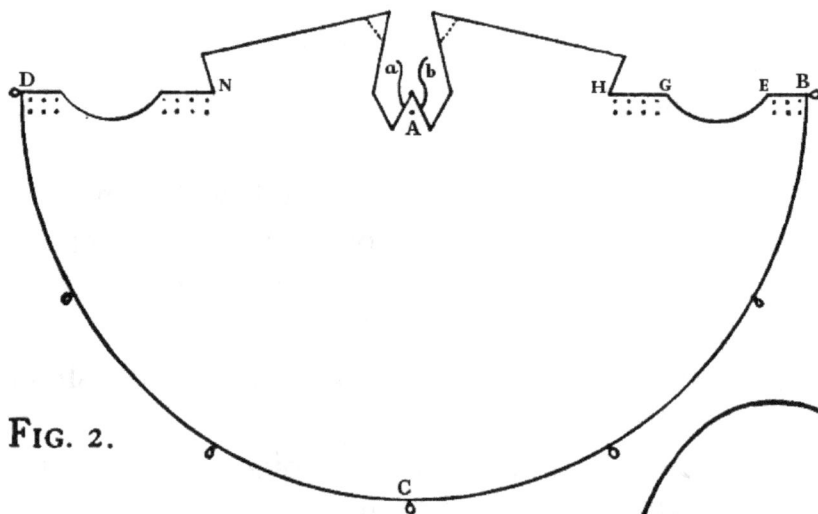

FIG. 2.

FIG. 3.

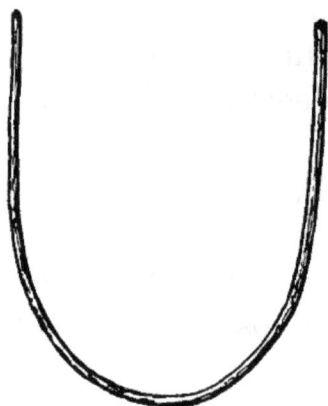

FIG. 4.

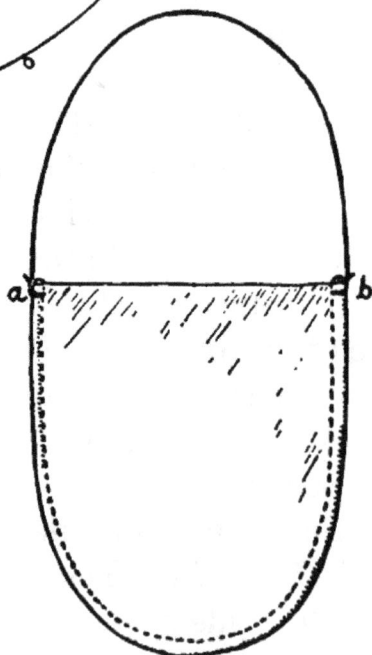

FIG. 5.

foot each. The depth of each segment, *Qd* and *Fe,* should be seven inches.

Above and below the door, between *H* and *B,* and *N* and *D,* make a double row of holes, three inches apart; they are for the lacing pins, and should be worked like button holes.

The thong, *ab,* is drawn through the triangular piece *A,* and tied or sewed fast.

All edges of the cover are now neatly hemmed.

Around the circular edge sew loops of canvas or stout cord to receive the tent pins; or better, get loops and eyes of some tent maker.

The cover will now appear as in Fig. 2.

For the frame, twelve poles will be needed. They should be twelve feet long and two and a half inches in diameter at the lower end, tapering slightly toward the top. The lower ends should be somewhat sharpened.

Lacing pins are ten inches long and one half inch thick. If cut green, they should be peeled of bark, except an inch near each end, Fig. 3.

For the door, bend a small green rod in the shape of a horseshoe, Fig. 4; cover with canvas, drawing edges over the rod and binding down, as in Fig. 5; at *a* and *b,* a cord is fastened to serve as a hinge.

SETTING UP THE TENT

There are two ways of setting up the tepee frame, called the three-pole and the four-pole ties. The three-pole tie, used by the Mandans, is perhaps the simpler.

Lay three poles on the ground as in Fig. 6, and bind firmly, two feet from the top.

The poles are set up in a tripod, Fig. 7, for the skeleton frame. Poles *A* and *B,* in front and spread apart, will inclose the door.

Positions of the other seven poles of the frame are shown in the ground diagram, Fig. 8. *A, B,* and *C* are the three poles of the skeleton frame. Poles *D, E,* and *F,* on the left, and *G, H,* and *I,* on the right, are raised in the order named. The rope or lariat *L,* Figs.

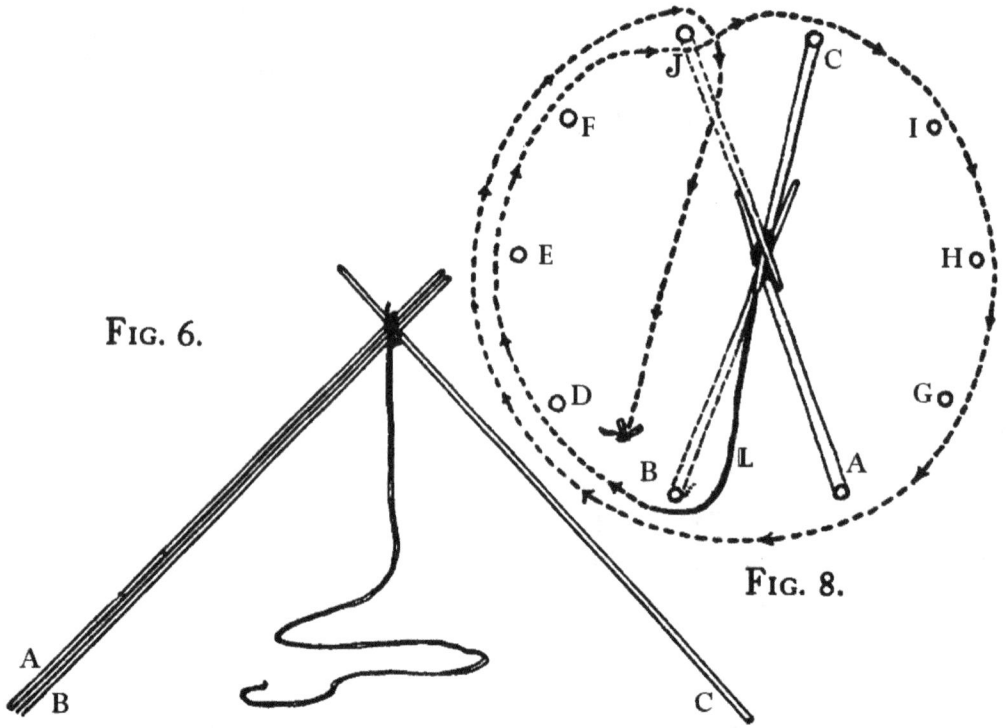

FIG. 6.

FIG. 8.

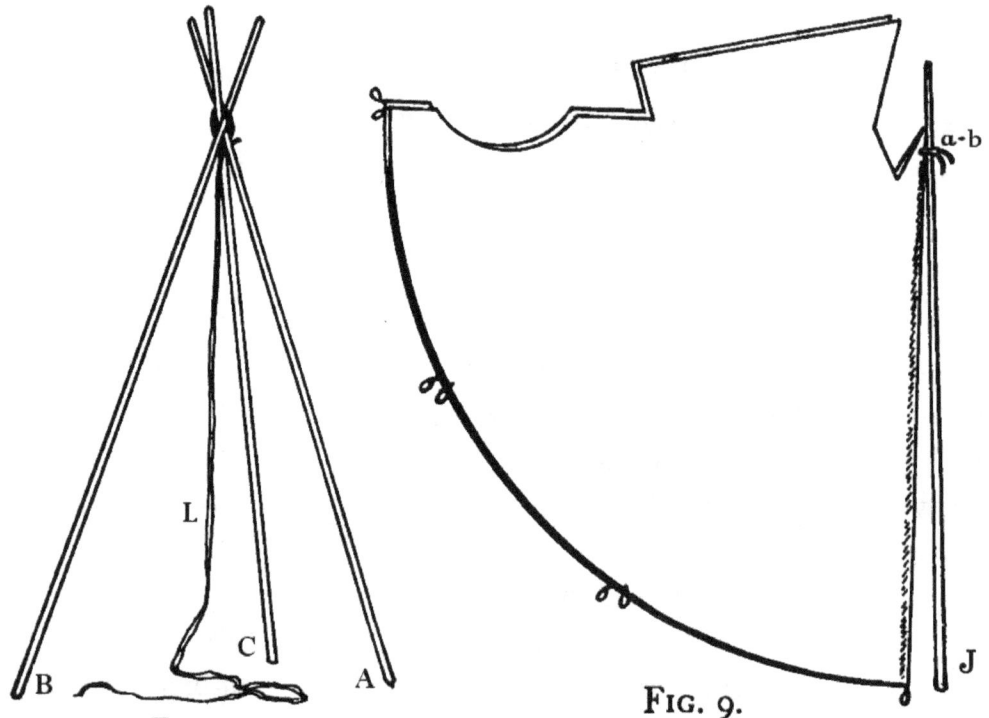

FIG. 7.

FIG. 9.

7 and 8, used for tying the skeleton frame, has been left hanging. This lariat is now drawn out through the door, between poles A and B, is carried quite around the frame, and is drawn tight about the tie.

The pole J in the rear of the tent is the last to be placed. On this pole the canvas cover is raised.

Lay the cover on the ground, weather side up, and fold once over. Lay down the pole J, and tie the cover to it by the cord ab, Fig. 9, two feet from the top.

Pole J with the cover is then raised in place between C and F. Before the cover is drawn, the lariat L is carried to the rear of the tent, around pole J, back into the tent again between J and C, and anchored firmly to a pin. Figure 10 shows the anchored frame. (Pole J is raised, but the tent cover is omitted in the figure.)

The tent cover is now drawn around the frame and laced. The loops at the lower edge of the cover are secured to the ground by tent pins, driven in aslant. The door is hung over one of the lacing pins.

Two poles are yet unused. They are raised and their upper ends are thrust into the pockets of the smoke flaps. By means of these poles, the smoke flaps may be propped down wind, so that the smoke may not be driven down the smoke hole. In wet weather, the smoke flaps may by the same means be folded over the smoke hole.

The tent, set up and ready, is shown in Fig. 11.

ANCHORING THE TENT

The object of pinning down the lariat L is to anchor the tent against the wind. The anchoring pin should be driven on the windward side of the fireplace.

The lariat may be anchored by one or two pins. A two-pin anchor is shown in Fig. 12.

FIG. 11.

FIG. 10.

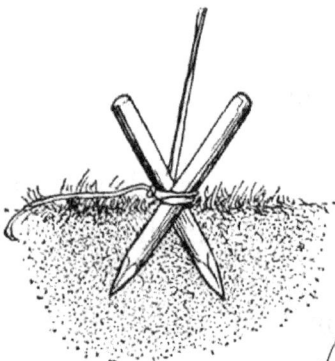

FIG. 12.

FIG. 13.

THE FIREPLACE

The fireplace is in the center of the tent, under the smoke hole. In summer, the fire may be made outside of the tent.

An Indian is rather sparing of fuel. Two or three sticks are laid each with an end in the fire; as the ends burn away, the sticks are pushed in. A small hot fire of coals results. When cooking is over, the sticks may be drawn apart and their ends buried in ashes. This keeps the coals alive for the next meal.

An Indian woman often keeps a goose or turkey wing to fan the fire, and brush the hearth clean.

A drying pole may be hung over the fire, lashed at either end to a tent pole. On this may be dried clothing, or shoes. The camp pot may be swung from it by a cord and a wooden hook, Fig. 13.

If cooking is done out of doors, a tripod is useful. Three saplings are bound together at the upper ends, and a wooden hook swung beneath, as in Fig. 14. By spreading the legs of the tripod, the pot may be lowered to any height.

In Figs. 15 and 16 are shown two ways of making a spit. Fig. 16 is much used by Indian hunters.

INSIDE OF THE TENT

Each member of an Indian family has his place in the tent to rest and sleep; for this reason, when a stranger comes to an Indian's tent, he stands waiting within the door, until the owner makes a place for him and invites him to sit down.

Figure 17 is the floor of a tent occupied by four boys. The floor is divided into sections, as an Indian would divide it.

In *A* are the pots, pans, and dishes, neatly covered with a cloth or paper. The water bucket should stand here, also covered.

In *B* all unused foods should be stored, in a box if possible.

C is the bed of the eldest boy. When not in use, blankets may be rolled up against the wall and serve for a seat.

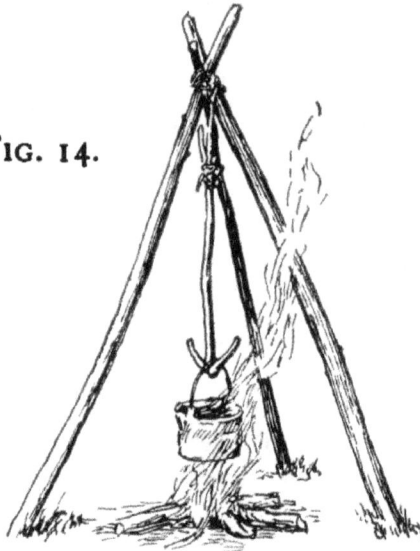

Fig. 14.

Fig. 15.

Fig. 16.

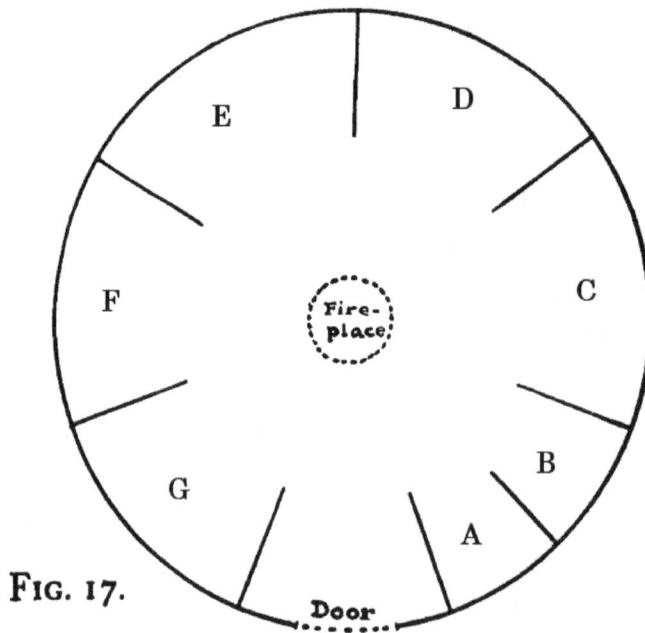

Fig. 17.

294

D is the bed of the second boy; *E,* of the third boy; *F,* of the youngest boy. Beds lie head to head, and foot to foot.

At *G,* wood is piled for the night, if the weather is stormy. In fair weather, the wood is piled outside.

If a guest is to be entertained, room should be made for him between *D* and *E;* for Indians hold the part of the tepee back of the fire to be the place of chief honor.

ARCHERY

No camp is complete without archery; but every boy should make his own bow and arrows.

A bow may be made of seasoned mulberry, ash, sassafras, or hickory. The bow staff should be straight, without knot or flaw. It should be four inches longer than the boy's own height.

Shave the bow into shape with a plane, making the back flat, the front round, as *a,* in Fig. 18. Cut nocks, *d,* Fig. 18, at the ends with a round file.

Against the flat back, in the very center of the bow, glue a small pine block, four inches long, shaped like *b,* Fig. 18, and stay it in place with a few wrappings of flax. Cover neatly with a piece of plush, sewed on or glued. This is for the handle.

Varnish, or rub with boiled linseed oil.

The completed bow is shown in *c,* Fig. 18.

THE BOWSTRING

The bowstring is made of thirty strands of shoemaker's thread. Take ten threads, wax with bees' wax and twist into a cord, *twisting from you.* When three such ten-stranded cords are made, twist them into one, *twisting toward you.* This will be your bowstring.

At one end, make a fixed loop, or eye, large enough to run easily on the upper arm of your bow. The other end of the string is tied

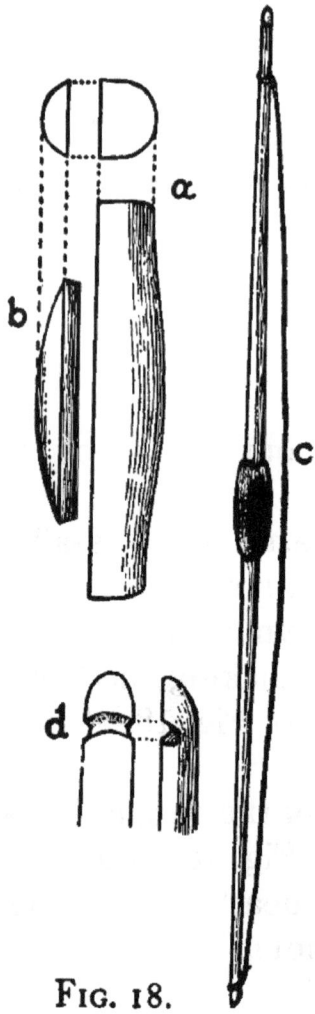

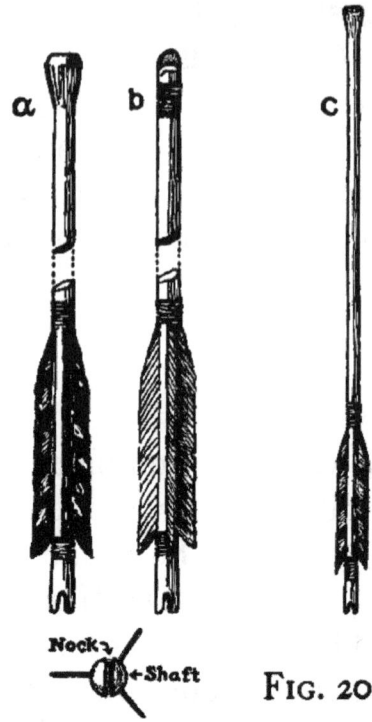

FIG. 20.

FIG. 18.

FIG. 19.

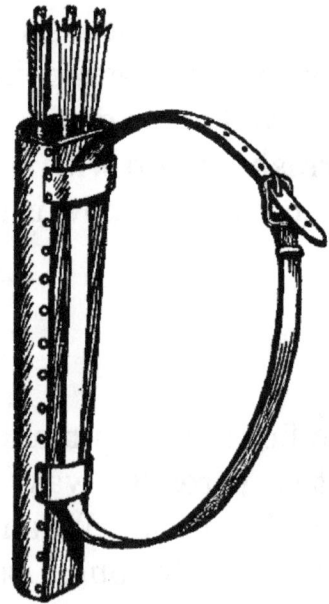

FIG. 21.

296

fast with a bowyer's knot, or timber hitch, Fig. 19.

The bowstring should be whipped with silk along the middle where it is drawn by the fingers. Keep your bowstring well waxed with bees' wax.

ARROWS

Arrows may be planed round, or shaved, from half inch strips of pine or hickory. They should be twenty-five or twenty-six inches long for boys, twenty-eight inches long for adults; and three eighths of an inch thick. The shaft must be straight.

The head may be left blunt; or the shaft may be split for a half inch, with a fine saw; and a bit of hoop iron may be inserted, and fixed with glue and a wrapping of fine wire. See *a* and *b,* Fig. 20.

There should be three feathers, taken from the same wing of a goose or turkey. Feathers may be cut from the shaft of the plume with a knife; or the aftershaft with its attached barbs may be stripped off with the fingers.

Glue feathers to the shaft of the arrow and trim evenly. A little silk and glue may be used to bind the upper and lower ends of the feathers to the shaft, *c,* Fig. 20.

A nock should be filed in the feather end of the shaft to receive the bowstring.

QUIVER

A good quiver is shown in Fig. 21. The back is made of a thin board, the floor of a half circular block; a piece of thick leather is nailed to the edges, with brass nails.

A belt passes over the right shoulder and under the left arm.

BRACING AND SHOOTING

To brace the bow, rest the lower end against the right foot; grasp the handle of the bow with the right hand, and push the eye of the bowstring into the nock with the left hand, Fig. 22.

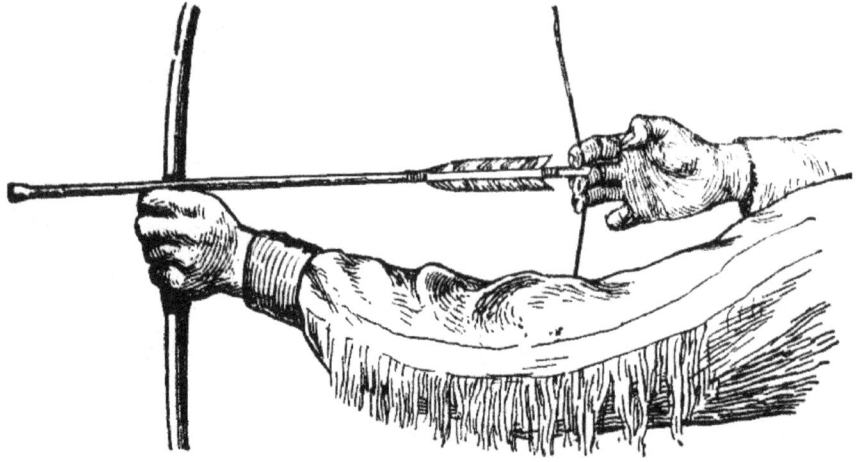

FIG. 23.

FIG. 24.

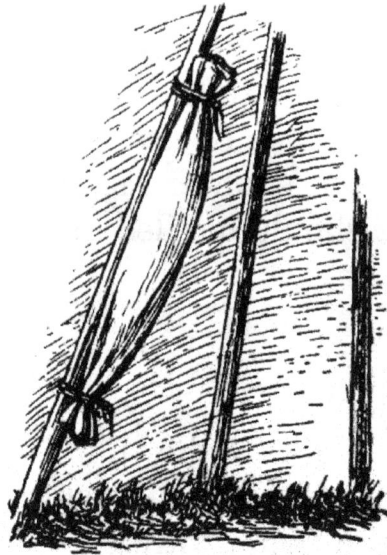

FIG. 22.

The arrow is laid on the bowstring, and drawn with the first three fingers of the right hand. The shaft is held between the first and second fingers, Fig. 23. Draw until the root of your thumb touches your right ear, and loose.

The arrow should be drawn on the left of the bow.

HINTS TO YOUNG CAMPERS

Do not throw away bits of refuse food; burn or bury them. Bury all tin cans.

Bury potatoes in sand or loose earth, to keep them fresh.

Air your bed clothing and blankets every day.

Bows and arrows, shoes, clothing, and the like may be stored out of the way by making them into a long bundle, and lashing them to one of the tent poles, as shown in Fig. 24.

Indians had no soap. Pots were scoured out with rushes. Your camp kettle and dishes may be cleaned in the same way; if no rushes can be found, use coarse grass, dipped in a little wet sand, and drench with water.

A camp in your back yard is nearly as good as one in the forest.